THE WELSH LINEAGE OF JOHN LEWIS

(1592-1657)

Emigrant to Gloucester, Virginia

Revised Edition

$\longleftarrow \Leftrightarrow \Rightarrow \longrightarrow$

GRACE MCLEAN MOSES

CLEARFIELD

Dedicated to my husband, MERILLAT MOSES, Colonel, U.S. Army(Retired), whose understanding, patience and general support contributed immensely to this effort. He, too, is a Welshman, descended through Einion Sais from Bleddyn ap Maenyrch, last native Lord of Brecknock.

First Edition, 1984

Revised Edition printed for
Clearfield Company, Inc. by
Genealogical Publishing Co., Inc.
Baltimore, Maryland
1992

Revised Edition reprinted for
Clearfield Company, Inc. by
Genealogical Publishing Co., Inc.
Baltimore, Maryland
1993, 1995, 1998, 2002

International Standard Book Number: 0-8063-4542-X

Made in the United States of America

THE WELSH LINEAGE OF JOHN LEWIS (1592-1657) EMIGRANT TO GLOUCESTER, VA.

By Grace McLean Moses, McLean, Virginia

In Colonial Virginia there were always a few prominent families in each county who held most of the civil and military offices for generations. In Gloucester County, Virginia, the foremost was that of LEWIS OF WARNER HALL. They were members of the King's Council, Colonels of the Militia and Vestrymen of Abingdon Parish. This family became one of the most distinguished in Virginia, and its descendants made many contributions, not only to the State, but to our national history.

The background of this illustrious family in the Old World has been in question for several centuries, and professional genealogists have attempted to resolve the lineage in Wales. A number of reputable genealogies have been published, but the most comprehensive and authoritative of these was that compiled by the late Merrow Edgerton Sorley in 1935.[1] Colonel Sorley certainly traced most of the later generations in much more detail than had ever been done before. However, he himself was not completely satisfied with his final effort; for the author corresponded with him before his untimely death in 1965, and he wrote her that he was aware of inaccuracies in his work, and that he hoped to publish a "Supplement" to correct them. Unfortunately, he passed away suddenly before that was possible.

The most notable error in Colonel Sorley's book was that of his proposing one *ROBERT LEWIS* as the immigrant ancestor of the Lewis Family of Warner Hall. He stated that his selection was purely "presumptive" and, according to him, based on "best evidence." At that time, this was all that was available. He brought forth the fact that there were *two* Robert Lewises who sailed from London to Virginia in 1635.[2]

---

[1] *"Lewis of Warner Hall, The History of a Family"* (1935), by Merrow Edgerton Sorley.

[2] *"Lists of Original Emigrants"* by John Camden Hotten, Pp. 79 and 103. (1874)

The earliest record of one Robert Lewis is in Norfolk County on March 15, 1640;[3] and another reference to a man of the identical name is in York County in 1644.[4] This last named Robert Lewis appears to have spent the remainder of his life within the bounds of York County; and after several other notations, he is appointed, with John Hansford, to make a Census of Hampton Parish on July 25, 1646. The final record of this man is a posthumous one in 1656, when, prior to September 30, 1656, he left a widow, Mary _____?_____ and two minor daughters, Mary and Alice. To these daughters he bequeathed 500 acres of land which he had purchased from John Roy, alias King, in November, 1649, in what was then York County, but soon became Gloucester. This land, situated on Poropotancke Creek (also Lewis Creek) was the foundation of the belief of Colonel Sorley that Robert Lewis of York County was the progenitor of the family of Warner Hall, as the latter family also owned land on Poropotancke Creek, although the two holdings were four or five miles apart. This area was just being "opened up" for Grants to new settlers. No doubt the similarity of names led Colonel Sorley astray, as he "assumed" that the land that Robert Lewis purchased on Poropotancke Creek was identical to that of the Plantation of *"Chimahocans" (or "Port Holy")* owned by Major William Lewis, who had purchased it from Colonel John West in 1658;[5] this last mentioned land was left by Major William Lewis to his heir, Major John Lewis, Jr. The latter made his home at "Chimahocans" (also called *Chemokins*) in New Kent County during his entire lifetime, and then he passed the estate to one of his sons, "Councillor" John Lewis of Warner Hall. The Robert Lewis land and the property of Major William Lewis were two distinct entities — as was also the land granted to John Lewis the Emigrant in 1653, also on Poropotancke Creek. Thus, the premise that Robert Lewis was the ancestor of Warner Hall, because of the proximity of the land, can be considered erroneous, in light of the facts.

Another error in *"Lewis of Warner Hall"* must be clarified before moving ahead with the Welsh research. In Chapter Thirty-five of this genealogy Colonel Sorley presents a Plate of a Lewis Coat-of-Arms,[6] "probably the most extensive ever used by a descendant of the Lewis family in this country." The Coat has twelve quarterings, with a shield of pretense. While placing the Lewis of Brecon Coat in the first and most

[3] *"Virginia Magazine of History and Biography"*, Vol. 41, P. 56.
[4] *"Ibid."*, Vol. 17, P. 211.
[5] *"Lewis of Warner Hall"*, P. 25.
[6] *"Lewis of Warner Hall"*, P. 858.

important quarter, it places the Coat of Lewis of the Van in the second quartering. This Coat was used by one Warner Lewis Olivier of Petersburg, Virginia, and an exactly similar one was used by Mrs. Austin R. Baldwin of New York City. It was believed, says Sorley, to have been compiled in England through research at the Royal College of Arms, and it has been in Mrs. Austin's family for about one hundred and fifty years. This Coat-of-Arms was most likely commissioned by descendants of the Warner Hall Family seeking to establish their background in Wales. Earlier in his genealogy Colonel Sorley mentions that a determined effort was made not too long ago to establish the Welsh ancestry of Robert Lewis of Virginia. A genealogist in England worked on the lineage and claimed it was the most difficult he had ever dealt with. Finally, he wrote: "Every Lewis in the Calendars of the Probate Court has been searched and the whole of the Brecon families been examined" — without definite success in establishing the connection. The only conclusion evolved was that "the descent from Lewis of the Van *may* be correct, as not another "Robert" of the proper date could be found."[7] It is apparent, now, that the College of Arms in London granted the above mentioned Coat-of-Arms on unsubstantiated evidence. The College of Arms, while being the ultimate authority on such matters in Great Britain, is not infallible, and has been known to make other errors in the past — it seems inevitable! However, the author does not believe that we can fault the College too harshly on this one point; for they had been given the *wrong ancestor in Virginia* to trace! But certainly they should not have granted the Coat-of-Arms to a pedigree not thoroughly and definitely verified.

Before pursuing the research, there is one more matter which must be clarified. In the Library of Congress the author found another publication of Colonel Sorley. It was published in 1965, immediately after his death. The book is entitled: "*Sorley Pedigree*"[8] and is a compilation of all his family lines in this country back into Europe, as far as 433 A.D. It was a considerable effort, but it is useless as a guide of the Warner Hall Family into its roots in Europe, because it names *ROBERT LEWIS* as the immigrant ancestor of the family and it goes back into Wales on the line of *LEWIS OF THE VAN* — which is the background Colonel Sorley stressed in his earlier work and which was generally believed *in 1935*. The new information was based on the discoveries of the tomb-

---

[7] "*Ibid.*", P. 20.

[8] "*Sorley Pedigree*", a compilation of the ancestry and descendants of Colonel Lewis Stone Sorley and Nan Merrow Sorley (1965). Pp. 53 and 54.

stones of the Lewis family in the ancient graveyard on Poropotancke Creek (in what is now King and Queen County) by Dr. Malcolm Harris and his compatriot, Mr. R. Tyler Bland; for without their curiosity, determination and dedication the matter would *never* have been resolved! Dr. Harris wrote in his article in *"The Virginia Magazine of History and Biography"* that he hoped a member of the Lewis Family would pursue the genealogy back into Wales, and that is the purpose of this research, with his blessing!

It is impossible to give too much credit to resolving the Pedigree of the Warner Hall Family to Dr. Harris, of West Point, Virginia; he and Mr. Bland, by pains-taking search unearthed several tombstones in an abandoned burying-site which proved to be the identical land of the original Grant of Land to the Immigrant ancestor in 1653. The findings were written up in two articles of *"The Virginia Magazine of History and Biography"* — in 1948 and 1954 — and were later published in the compilation of *"Genealogies of Virginia Families"*, Volume IV, Pp. 200-224. Beyond any reasonable doubt the first two generations of this family lie in this graveyard.

The first tomb, discovered in 1948, was that of *JOHN LEWIS.*

It read —

> "Here lieth interred the body of John Lewis (borne in Munmoth shire) died the 21st of August 1657 aged 63 years. The anagram of his name I shew no ill".

Moreover, the tombstone of John Lewis, as well as that of his grandson, Captain Edward Lewis, had engraved thereon a Coat-of-Arms which proved of immeasurable help in identifying the lineage back into Wales; for strict rules were in effect at that time governing the use of Heraldic Arms. Colonel Sorley was correct about one thing, however; in his *"Lewis of Warner Hall"* on page 18 he wrote: *"It may be asserted without fear of contradition that the emigrant Lewis who went to Virginia was a member of some branch of the Lewis family of Brecon."* He made this judgment on the basis of markings on old silver which had been in the Lewis family for generations and on general tradition and heresay! That was a valid opinion then, but since that time there has been brought forth more concrete evidence — beginning with the wonderful discoveries of Dr. Harris and Mr. Bland!

Realizing that JOHN LEWIS was the man we were seeking, we turned to the Virginia *"Land Patent Books"* (as had Dr. Harris) and we verified: *"Mr. Jon Lewis*, 250 acres at the head of a branch belonging to Poroptanke Creek, called Lewis Creek, but formerly Totopotomoys Creek in

Gloucester County. *July 1, 1653,* etc. Transported 5 persons: Jon Lewis, Lida Lewis, Wm. Lewis, Edward Lewis, Jon Lewis, Jr."[9] John Lewis paid the passage of four other persons and himself, and the land granted to him for these "Headrights" (50 acres per person) was identical to that of the ancient graveyard. When John Lewis arrived in Virginia in the year 1653, he was an old man of about sixty years of age. Due to the paucity of records of that time in the "burned out" counties involved, it is difficult to be exact about the relationships of this group of people. However, the author would like to make some deductions and assumptions concerning them. The Head of the family was, of course, JOHN LEWIS THE EMIGRANT. The William Lewis mentioned in the Grant of 1653 came out in later records quite early as MAJOR WILLIAM LEWIS. Judging from his title one would expect him to be a man of "middle age", and the title could well have been earned in England or Wales in the Civil War, as he used it immediately upon arrival in Virginia in a grant of land for 50 acres in York County.[10] He was also a man with considerable means for he proceeded to purchase over 10,000 acres of land in about five years. He was also active in the affairs of the Colony, taking part in plans for "Western Expansion."[11] He appears to have died between 1658 and 1667.[12] The name Lida is as yet not accounted for, but the author proposes that she was the wife of Major William Lewis. It seems logical that John Lewis, Jr. (also mentioned among the Headrights of John Lewis the Elder) was the older of the two young men who came with the Emigrant; for he obtained his first Land Grant in 1655, and if that year was the year of his majority, he would have been born about 1633/34, in Wales. There must have been a family relationship between Major William Lewis and John Lewis, Jr., for the latter was the heir to "Port Holy," the plantation purchased by the former from Colonel John West. Also, traveling with the Emigrant and bearing the same name, denotes a close family tie. The "Port Holy" estate went to a son of John Lewis, Jr. — namely "Councillor"-John Lewis of Warner Hall — thus cementing the "line" from John Lewis the Emigrant to the Warner Hall Family. John Lewis, Jr., was a Vestryman of St. Peter's Parish, New Kent County, and a "Major" in the County Militia. His tombstone has never been discovered, so that exact date of his death is unknown. He married one Isabella Miller, daughter of

9 "Land Patent Book No. 3", P. 4.
10 *"York County Deed Book No. 3",* P. 59.
11 *"Journals of the House of Burgesses" (1619-1659),* P. 106.
12 *"Lewis of Warner Hall",* P. 26.

James Miller the elder of York County,[13] and the sister of James Miller, Jr., whose heir she became. Her tombstone is among those at the graveyard. The other young man with the Emigrant, one *Edward Lewis*, has been lost to view by most Virginia genealogists, but the author suggests that perhaps he was the Edward Lewis who, together with one Thomas Robinson, received a Land Grant of 1,140 acres in Rappahannock County on February 20, 1662. This would indicate that Edward Lewis reached his majority about 1662; hence, he was probably born about 1641 in Wales. Also, the Will of Humphrey Booth of November, 1665, in Rappahannock County[14] mentions a bequest to *"Edward, the son of Edward Lewis"* of "two cows"; this was the contemporary manner of honoring family relationships. The deduction is that Edward Lewis married a daughter of Humphrey Booth and had a son, Edward.

Before we leave the scene of the Lewis Family in New Kent County on Poropotancke Creek, the author must digress and note another inaccuracy which has been circulated about the Warner Hall Lineage. Mr. John Manahan of Charlottesville, Virginia, sent in an article on this subject to the "Notes and Queries" Section of the *"Virginia Magazine of History and Biography"*, Volume 15(1957), pages 108 and 109, in which he traced the line of John Lewis of Gloucester County back to the Parish of Llantilio Pertholey in Monmouthshire, Wales. He based his search on the name *"Port Holy"* given to the Plantation of Major William Lewis and inherited by John Lewis, Jr. About this "clue", Mr. Manahan was correct — for the lineage indicates that parish. However, he proceeded to "hook on" the Emigrant to the family of one Dr. David Lewis, a very prominent person in the Admiralty during Queen Elizabeth's reign and a native of Abergavenny, claiming that the family name was in reality *WALLIS* (from the Norman *de Valence*) and that the true Coat-of-Arms of our Gloucester Family was that of "Wallis." He added that this Coat-of-Arms belonged to the family of de Cantaloupe (Overlords of the Dr. David Lewis family in Abergavenny). This, of course, was pure speculating; for the Emigrant *must have known* the Arms of his father, and no gentleman of that period would have used the arms of another family — in fact, there was a punishment for such a mis-use! So we must forget Mr. Manahan's "theories" and return to the search for the truth! The Arms of the David Lewis Family were: *"Chequy or and sable, on a*

---

[13] *"Tyler's Historical Quarterly Magazine"*, Volume I, P. 285.
[14] *"Wills of Rappahannock County (1664-71)"*, P. 45; also noted in *"Genealogies of Virginia Families"*, Volume V, P. 633.

fesse gules three leopards' heads jessant-de-lys of the first. "[15] One can easily ascertain the complete difference between these Arms and those engraved on the tombstone in Gloucester.

It was evidently most important to the Emigrant John Lewis to perpetuate for his descendants the true background of his family in Wales; for the tombstones had to be ordered at great cost of time and expense from England and the action clearly shows the social standing of this family in the old country, as well as in Virginia. Also, please remember that the Welsh have always laid great importance on the Coat-of-Arms which a family bore — often the surnames changed in a pedigree, but true descent was always traced through the Coat.

Aside from the Lewis of Brecon Arms (about which there has never been any doubt) the graves in Gloucester County had other quarterings on the shield. Next to the *LEWIS* Arms was that of the Prince of Caerlleon, the *HOWELL* FAMILY, and their Coat has always been *"Gules, three towers tripled-towered Argent."* These two Coats are very well-identified, but there is some doubt concerning the third and fourth quarterings on the shield. Dr. Malcolm Harris stated in his article that Mrs. Littleton Fitzgerald of Richmond had interpreted the engravings on the tombstones for him;[16] she said that the third quartering (*"Argent three Chevronels Gules"*) was unidentified, and that the fourth quartering was *"Argent three torteaux."* At that time the third quartering certainly was not identified, but it is impossible to identify a Coat without the tinctures being known, which, of course, they could not possibly be from a stone engraving. As to the "three torteaux", "they," again, were subject to the tinctures, different names denoting different colors, and they, in turn, describing different family arms, making an entirely different interpretation. Only a thorough research on the genealogy of the "Rhys Goch" Line of Brecon could ever identify the third and fourth quarterings of the Lewis shield, and at that point of time no one knew the truth about the Lewis family genealogy. This is a complicated shield, and surely the man who had it engraved on the tombstone understood his lineage perfectly. The three quarterings would indicate that three heiresses had married into the Rhys Goch Line — heiresses of such prominence that their Coat-of-Arms warranted being included on the shield of that family.

Realizing from the Coat-of-Arms that this family was rooted in Wales, the author wrote to the Bishop of Wales, the Right Reverend

---

[15] *"History of Monmouthshire"* by Bradney, Vol. I, Part II, P. 285.

[16] *"Genealogies of Virginia Families",* Vol. IV, P. 212.

7

John Richard Worthington Peale-Hughes,[17] at his Cathedral at Cardiff, asking his advice and assistance in the search being undertaken for the forebears of JOHN LEWIS OF VIRGINIA, who bore as his family's Coat-of-Arms *"A dragon's head erased vert, holding in its mouth a sinister hand gules."* The Bishop replied that there were quite a few families of the name of LEWIS in existence in Monmouthshire; so he very kindly passed the query on to the Herald Extraordinary of Wales, Major Francis Jones, who, being ill at that time, gave it to a professional genealogist working at the National Library of Wales at Aberystwyth, Dyfed, Wales. This gentleman, Mr. Basil G. Twigg, undertook the first phase of the research, as he was an expert in the subject of "Patronymics" — even lecturing to Family History Societies on the subject. The "Patronymics" system is a peculiarity to Welsh History and Genealogy. For centuries there were no surnames; a son took as his surname the first name of his father, usually, with the word "ap" in between. A daughter did the same, using "vz" or "verch", instead. This complicated the research for the author considerably, until Mr. Twigg explained the system in great detail. It was not possible to group persons together as families and to identify them with a common surname. The element most powerful in Welsh Genealogy was the Coat-of-Arms,[18] and that was exceedingly useful in tracing the background of John Lewis the Emigrant to Virginia; for on his tombstone was engraved the Arms of the illustrious *RHYS GOCH ("the red-haired"), Lord of Ystrad-Yw and Ewyas.* The antecedents of Rhys Goch were the Lords of Brecknock, established in that area for centuries. The Parish was *Llanelly.* They finally settled for the surname of LEWIS, in the male line (the *only* continuous male line from Rhys Goch).[19] Thus the research moved into Wales, where it proved to be a challenge, an inspiration, and a justification of the record of the family in Virginia; for JOHN LEWIS, buried in the ancient graveyard in King and Queen County, transplanted to Colonial Virginia the "stock" of the Lewis Family of Llanelly, Breconshire — and there is small wonder that they prospered in the New World, for they brought with them *the best blood in Wales to "adventure" in Virginia!*

While waiting for a Report from Mr. Twigg, the author decided to do something on her own to further the research. Working on the premise of Mr. Manahan's article about "Llantilio Pertholey," she wrote to the

---

[17] Letter of June 2, 1980.
[18] *"The History of Monmouthshire"* (1906) by Sir Joseph Alfred Bradney.
[19] *"Ibid.",* Volume I, Pt. II, P. 289.

Vicar of the ancient Church of St. Teilo — which is the heart of the Parish of Llantilio Pertholey. Historically, it is known as *St. Teilo in the Bright Bush,* and it was founded in the sixth century by King Iddon. of Gwent. The first church has long since gone, but in the thirteenth century it was re-built in Romanesque-style stone — which still stands, although there was a fire in 1974; but the church was beautifully restored and is one of the truly lovely and impressive "relics" of that part of Wales. The author requested the Vicar, the Reverend Donald Francis, to transcribe all the *"Lewis"* entries from his *"Register"* — if it went back to the last part of the sixteenth century. He most carefully copied these for her, beginning with the first year's entries for 1591/92 — up to the year 1640, after which the entries in the *"Register"* became incomplete. There was a gap from 1645-1660. The *"Register"* was a copy of an original which had been made in the latter part of the Eighteenth Century. However, we are most fortunate that it is *extant,* as there are very few Church registers still in existence for the period involved for the northwest part of Monmouthshire. Parish registers in England and Wales form a most important and indispensable source for records of this period. I shall be forever grateful to the Vicar of St. Teilo's for his carefulness, his kindness and his courtesy in doing this wonderful thing for the family of John Lewis. Without his help nothing would have been possible!

About six months after the "entries" came from St. Teilo, Mr. Twigg forwarded to the author a copy of a WILL of one *RICHARD LEWIS OF LLANGATOCK CRICKHOWELL, GENT.,* in Breconshire, dated 15 March, 1627, and proved 18 April, 1628. He wrote: *"I would be very surprised if this were not the will we are looking for!"*[20] Both he and and the author were in agreement that this was indeed the true family of John Lewis of Virginia! Shortly before receiving Mr. Twigg's letter with the WILL of Richard Lewis, the author received a packet from Mr. R.W. McDonald, Keeper of Manuscripts and Records at the National Library of Wales; it contained quite a few Xerox excerpts from published material on the Rhys Goch Line — which would indicate that, on the basis of the tombstones in Virginia and the Coat-of-Arms engraved thereon, this gentleman did not doubt that the author was researching the lineage of Rhys Goch. Included in the packet was material from the well-known authority on Breconshire, one Theophilus Jones, who compiled the accepted *"History"*[21] on that part of Wales. With this informa-

---

[20] Letter of Basil G. Twigg of December 28, 1982.

[21] *"History of Breaknockshire",* Theophilus Jones, 4 Vols. (1909)

tion in hand it seemed very certain that the WILL which Mr. Twigg had sent later was the correct one. Mr. McDonald was a wonderful help.

Mr. Twigg pointed out that the Testator of the will, Richard Lewis, was using the "Patronymic" system in his WILL. His sons were named as (1) *LEWIS* (who appeared to be deceased, as he was not mentioned except through his children); (2) *EDWARD PRICHARD* and (3) *THOMAS PRICHARD*. Mr. Twigg stated that Prichard was the patronymic for *"ap Richard", or "son of Richard."* Accepting this procedure, then the son, LEWIS, would have been *LEWIS PRI-CHARD*. Theophilus Jones in his *"History"* gives only the eldest son, presumably, one *WILLIAM LEWIS* who appears to be dead for the "heir" of the Richard Lewis of Will 1627 is one *RICHARD*, a young grandson, apparently, as his guardian is his Uncle Edward Prichard, also named as the Executor of the Will. Mr. Twigg thought that all the children (grandchildren) named in the Will with the surname LEWIS were *"certainly children of the testator's son LEWIS"* although further research by the author proved this interpretation incorrect. These children were [1]*"Thomas Lewis"*, one of the sons of son Lewis; [2]*"Maudelen Lewis"* (probably a grandchild, daughter of Lewis); [3]*"Marie Lewis"*, grandchild (probably a daughter of son Lewis); [4]*"Doritie Lewis"* (probably a daughter of Lewis); [5]*"Elizabeth Lewis"* (probably a daughter of Lewis, although possibly a grandaughter). Then followed — *"Elizabeth Lewis"*, daughter (sic), and *last but not least* finally [6]*"To grandchild JOHN LEWIS — 4 sheep, 4 lambs, and a filly."* This WILL definitely proves that Richard Lewis (Will 1627/28) had a son LEWIS who had a son JOHN. With the patronymic system in use JOHN LEWIS could only be interpreted as *"John the son of Lewis."* Towards the end of this letter, Mr. Twigg wrote: "While the mystery of how John Lewis actually fits with the Breconshire family and Llantilio Pertholey, Monmouth-shire, *circumstantial evidence for the connection grows stronger."*

Upon receiving this WILL with his comments from Mr. Twigg, the author sent him immediately (early in the following January) the Xerox copies of the "Entries" from the "Register" of St. Teilo's which the Vicar of that church had forwarded to her six months before. He did not seem aware of the existence of the *"Register"*, but was most interested, and requested that I ask the Vicar to send him photostatic copies of the years of the *"Register"* from 1591 to 1600, which the Vicar did at the author's suggestion and expense. Then Mr. Twigg asked to be allowed to go to St. Teilo's and personally examine the *"Register"*, which he did for one whole afternoon; and, upon his return to Aberystwyth, he forwarded several entries which he considered "possibilities." We were looking for a child baptized at St. Teilo's about 1594 (according to the tombstone in Gloucester County, Virginia), named "John Lewis" — who came from the line of Rhys Goch in Breconshire. We always had to bear in mind the possibility of the use of the patronymic system of nomenclature which was just then changing into the English custom of surnames — sometimes, both were used in the same family. It was quite confusing. Also, to be considered were the use of colloquialisms in the country parishes. Lastly, Mr. Twigg had instructed the author that "dates" in that period were not to be taken too exactly, and that about two years either side of any given date might be a "possibility."

Using the WILL from Brecknockshire and the entries from St. Teilo together, it was possible to work out the next two generations of the family of Richard Lewis of Llangattock Crickhowell, Brecon. We were blessed with the fact that the *"Register"* started in the exact year of the baptism of a *"JOHN, SON OF LEWIS RYCKETTS"* on February 22, 1591/92 (the baptismal "font" was ancient — pre-Norman); Mr. Twigg stated that the "Rycketts" could very well be a "colloquialism" of "Richards"; in other words, Lewis Rycketts could quite likely be "Lewis ap Richard". Here we find a John Lewis (son of Lewis, as in the WILL) baptized in the year 1592 (two years from the date on the tombstone), in Llantilio Pertholey Parish, and of Monmouthshire, Wales — as stated on the tombstone in Virginia! Further on in the *"Register"* Mr. Twigg found the marriage of *JOHN LEWIS PRICKET* (probably a colloquialism of Richard) *AND JOHANE LEWIS OF LLANTILIO PERTHOLEY* on February 3, 1610 (the author had brought this marriage to Mr. Twigg's attention from among the entries which the Vicar had sent). The Vicar had copied only the "L" entries for LEWIS (for those are what she had requested), he did not copy any "P" or "R" entries, such as this marriage would come under, and only included it because the bride was named "Lewis." Mr. Twigg wrote that "young" marriages were the order of the day. Also, John Lewis Pricket would mean in the patronymic system — *JOHN, THE SON OF LEWIS, THE GRANDSON OF RICHARD;* this was exactly what he was in the WILL of his grandfather in 1627/28. Lastly, Mr. Twigg noted in the *"Register"* the death of one *"CATHERINE RICHARD buried September 29, 1615"* and of one *"LEWIS PRICHARD buried on May 4, 1616."* Here we have all the variations of the patronymic system — "Pricket" (the colloquialism of Richard) and Richard (for Lewis' father's first name) and Catherine Richard (taking her husband's last name). This appears to be the transitional stage in Wales and is definitely the most difficult with which to work. The three children of John and Johane Lewis were baptized at St.

11

Teilo's as (1) *Gwenllian,* on February 5, 1611; (2) *Lettus* (another "colloquialism" for Lettyce, a popular name in a prominent family of this area) on March 1, 1615; and *Watkin* on January 1, 1621. Finally, there was a baptism of *"JOHN, SON OF JOHN LEWIS ON DECEMBER 15, 1633".* Going back in this article one will note that 1633/34 was the date of birth the author had deduced for John Lewis, Jr., of Virginia (the older of the two young men with John Lewis the Emigrant, based solely on the date of 1655 when he received his first Land Grant, supposedly on reaching his majority). The author had requested Mr. Twigg to especially look for this date — and he came up with December 15, 1633! John Lewis' other relative, *EDWARD LEWIS,* was not noted in the *"Register",* probably because it became incomplete after 1640, and the baptism of Edward Lewis should have been about 1641 (judging from the date he received *his* first Land Grant). Furthermore, it appears that the patronymic system seems to have been abandoned by 1633, *when John Lewis Pricket became John Lewis.* Please note that here we appear to have the two connecting generations between the established line of Rhys Goch (indicated on the tombstone in Virginia) down to the last published member of that family — Richard Lewis of Llangattuck Crickhowell — to his son LEWIS (mentioned in Richard's WILL) — to the baptism of Lewis' son JOHN LEWIS (in 1591/92) in Llantilio Pertholey (Please remember that in Virginia a Lewis family plantation was named "Port Holy"). Added to these facts, is the Pedigree of the Lewis of Llanelly family as recorded in the newly published genealogy written by Mr. Peter C. Bartrum, who is the acknowledged authority on Welsh Genealogy; Mr. Bartrum very kindly offered to allow the National Library of Wales (which was preparing his latest book for publication) to send the author page No. 1544 of same — as it covered the most recent information on the known descendants of Rhys Goch, both in the Llangeny and Llanelly lines. At the end of both lines in the pedigree he had written an arrow pointing to "Mons." (Monmouthshire). Evidently Mr. Bartrum had arrived at the same conclusion that the present research revealed — namely, that the line of Rhys Goch went down into Monmouthshire.

There is one other point which should be made clear at this time. In his first Report Mr. Twigg went into great detail concerning the interpretation of the arms of John Lewis of Virginia. He agreed that the first quartering was that of Rhys Goch; the second was most likely that of Howell of Caerlleon; the third was not as yet known; and the "fourth was undoubtedly that of the *wife* of John Lewis, as shown by its position on the shield." This Coat was "of three plates." Mrs. Fitzgerald interpreted it as "torteaux", but, as the genealogy was developed, it appeared that Johane Lewis was probably a descendant of the family of the Dr. David Lewis brought forward by Mr. Manahan in 1957. Dr. David Lewis had no heirs; however, his brother William left heirs. This family was *LEWIS OF LLANDDEWI RHYDDERCH* and *LLANDDEWI YSGYRID* in Monmouthshire, and they were descended on the distaff side from one Sir Walter de Trevely, a Norman Knight who came into Wales with Bernard de Newmarsh shortly after the Norman Conquest of England. In those times Sir Walter owned most of the Parish of Llanddewi Rhydderch, and he bore as his arms — *"Azure three plates."* The "plates" are always of a silver color (Argent). This Coat is the fourth quartering on the arms of John Lewis of Virginia. The family ran out in the male lines, and a female married into the family of *de Valence* (Wallis) mentioned in the article by Mr. Manahan. They bore an entirely different Coat-of-Arms from the Rhys Goch Line, but they finally settled for the surname of LEWIS about the same time. It, too, was an illustrious line—going back on the distaff side to *WILLIAM THE MARSHAL,* Earl of Pembroke and Striguil, supporter of four reigns of Plantagenet Kings, who was known in his lifetime as "the greatest knight of Europe." Johane's father was one William Lewis the elder of Ysgyrid Parish*(right next to Llantilio Pertholey and Llanddewi Rhydderch) and her mother was Elizabeth Proger of Wern-ddu — of the oldest and most famous of the families of Monmouthshire, namely, *the Senior Line of HERBERT.* In Welsh, Herbert is said to mean "Hir" (tall) and "Pert" (handsome). Johane was from the same line as the famous Dr. David Lewis previously noted. This Lewis family had for some time owned much land in the Parish of Llantilio Pertholey; Sir Robert Wallis and his son William were Lords of the Manor *Triley* in early times, a manor on the slope of the Deri Mountain. There is a private Chapel in the Church of St. Teilo called "The Triley Chapel", dedicated in their honor. Their Coat-of-Arms was quartered with the Arms of de Trevely and are emblazoned as such on the East window of the Church of Llanddewi Rhydderch. There is a "Lewis Chapel in the Church of Abergavenny where the great-grandfather of Johane Lewis — Lewis ap John (Wallis) was the Vicar of both Abergavenny and Llantilio Pertholey.

The Coat on the second quartering of the shield of John Lewis has always been known — that of Howell of Caerlleon; but perhaps it would be worthwhile to relate "how" it came on the Rhys Goch Arms. The son of Rhys Goch, one Genillin (Cynhyllyn) married Jenet, daughter of Sir Howel of Caerlleon. A *Grant of Arms* was given to him in the eleventh

---

* See Supplement.

century;[22] and Bradney reiterated this connection in the Pedigree of Maenyrch[23] in his *"History"*. There can be no question of its authenticity.

The only other "unidentified" Coat of the engraving (according to Mrs. Fitzgerald) is that of the third quarter — *three Chevronels*. The author proposes that this Coat is that of the de Turberville family of Crickhowell in Brecon. It would have been added to the Lewis shield by the marriage of the father of Richard Lewis of Llangattuck Crickhowell — indeed, it was the Coat of the mother of the said Richard Lewis — a family who owned the Castle of Crickhowell and who lived in the same parish of Llanelly. The father of Richard Lewis, one *LEWIS AP THOMAS,* married *MAUD*, the daughter of Thomas Lewis John ap Gwilym, Lord of Turberville and Coytie.[24] This line goes back to Sir Payne Turberville, who came into Wales with Bernard de Newmarsh shortly after the Norman Conquest. Third in descent from this Sir Payne the Norman, another Sir Payne married one *Mavd,* daughter and sole heiress to *MORGAN GAM* who was a nephew to *JESTYN AP GWRGAN, PRINCE OF GLAMORGANSHIRE*[25] and ancestor to one of the Five Royal Tribes of Wales. The arms of Jestyn were *"Gules three Chevronels Argent."*[26] The next in the Turberville Line, one Sir Gilbert Turberville, quartered his Turberville Arms with those of Jestyn ap Gwrgan, henceforth. Actually, the blood of Jestyn was crossed with the line of Rhys Goch on several other occasions, as shown by the pedigrees of Mr. Bartrum in his genealogies. So, it appears that the Coat-of-Arms of John Lewis of Virginia has been fully explained.

Before leaving the matter of the Coat, the subject of the "origin" of the Coat should be considered. Colonel Sorley went into this subject in his *"Lewis of Warner Hall,"*[27] and set forth two interpretations which had been put into circulation at various times. One related to a hunting incident connected with Llewellyn, Prince of Wales, and the other to the settlement of Ireland by invading warriors. The author related these two explanations when she corresponded with Dr. Michael Siddons, the Heraldic authority in Wales (whose latest book is being prepared for

---

[22] Letter from Dr. Michael Siddons, outstanding authority on Welsh "Heraldry", dated 5 June, 1983, giving the citation of the Grant as *Cardif Manuscript 2-38, f. 40.*

[23] *"The History of Monmouthshire",* Volume I, Part II, Page 338.

[24] *"History of Monmouthshire",* page 338.

[25] *"The Llyfr Baglan",* by John Williams, Edited in 1910 by Bradney, page 276.

[26] *"Ibid."* page 310n.

[27] *"Lewis of Warner Hall"* page 856.

publication by the National Library). Dr. Siddons had asked for these Virginia "stories", as he stated that he had never in Wales heard of any explanation for the origin of the arms of Rhys Goch. At the same time the author sent to Dr. Siddons a verification which her own research had developed. In *"The Heraldic Visitation of Wales"* is an account of the granting of arms to one *Llewellyn ap Ynyr, of Ial, or Yale, in Denbighshire.* "This chieftain, 'by his valour in Battle, obtained from his Prince, Gryffydd ap Madoc, Lord of Dinas Bran, the honorable distinction in his arms of four bloody strokes, or in the heraldic phrase, paly eight or and gules. For, while he was talking to his Prince after the fight, with his left hand smeared with blood, he accidently drew it across his sword, and left on it the mark of his four fingers. The Prince, observing this, ordered him to carry them on his shield; and at the same time bestowed on him the township of Gelligynan in the neighborhood, as a more substantial mark of his favor.' "[28] There is justification for this interpretation of the Rhys Goch Arms, in that the four bloody fingers on the sword were, of necessity, of the left hand, and all descriptions of the Lewis Arms indicate a *"sinister"* bloody hand. Llewellyn was of the family of *YNYR*, descended from a British King of Gwent of the sixth century. Another fact which strengthens the assumption that this is the origin of the Lewis Coat-of-Arms is the mentioning in the Grant of Llewellyn as "of Ial." This place is again mentioned in the authoritative genealogy by Mr. Peter C. Bartrum[29] when he writes at the bottom of page one of the Rhys Goch Pedigree — *"Eglwys Iail equals Llangynider, Ystrad-yw."* This reference concludes this genealogy of *Genillin Ap Rhys Goch* — so it would obviously connect the "place" with the "pedigree" of the family. Incidentally, Genillin is the descendent of Rhys Goch from whom the Lewis Family descends. Also, it would indicate to the author that Mr. Bartrum believes that Yale is in the "land" of Ystrad-Yw, (Herefordshire) the Lordship of Rhys Goch. The "land" and the "blood" seem to be firmly joined. Another connection of the "Coat", "Place" and "Land" occurs in the Pedigree of *Genillin ap Rees Goch lo. of Llangenider eglwys yayle* in the "Pedigree of Mynarch, Lord of Brecknock", his grandfather.[30] Coats-of-Arms in Wales are never borne by the famous ancestor of the line, but developed through the years by valorous exploits of descendants, and these arms were borne by succeeding generations descended from that famous ancestor — such as RHYS GOCH.

---

[28] *"Heraldic Visitation of Wales"* (1843) by Lewis Dwnn, Vol. II, P. 232n.
[29] *"Welsh Genealogies"* (1974) by Peter C. Bartrum, Vol. 4, P. 806.
[30] *"Llyfr Baglan"*, by John Williams, Edited by Bradney (1910), P. 111.

Much detailed consideration has been given in this article to an analysis of the Coat-of-Arms of John Lewis for several reasons. First of all, it was the lode-star that led us to the pedigree, the lineage, and the family of John Lewis. The Coat, in Welsh History and Genealogy, is the most important element present. It is, in essence, the ancestor, the descendants, and the family denominator. In Brecknock, it is especially important. In *"The Llyfr Baglan"* John Williams wrote: *"Brec.sheire men all ge n'allie are the beast Recorders of Pedigrees and other ancient p'sidents that I know in anye countrey."*[31]

Rodney Dennys, the Herald of the Royal College of Arms, wrote in his recently published book: "It is reasonable to think that several of the Welsh Princes and Princelings, in the lands bordering on the marshes, probably adopted armorial devices during the twelfth century, and a few remaining seals from the later years of that century support this. Many more from the thirteenth century remain in evidence, and from the next century onward armorial bearings were in general use throughout Wales."[32]

Major Francis Jones, former Herald Extraordinary of Wales, wrote: "The structure of Welsh society from very early times was essentially aristocratic, and it remained so until the destruction by Henry VIII of the legal concept that buttressed it. The Welsh theory was that no one could be a freeman, inherit property, enjoy privileges, or be received into the community, unless he could prove an agnatic ancestry for a certain number of generations."[33]

From these excerpts it is possible to understand that "bloodlines" were of the utmost importance to a Welshman of this period. Hence, it is possible to envision *why* John Lewis went to such pains to perpetuate his family background in the wilds of a New World.

Finally, a word concerning the "motto" which is said to be "Omne Solum Forti Patria Est" — "Every Land is Home to a Brave Man." This motto has been thought to belong to the Lewis of Warner Hall Family, although Dr. Siddons, the heraldic authority in Wales, was unaware of the existence of such a motto;[34] so the author would assume that this motto had been granted and placed on the shield of "Lewis" simultaneously with the granting of the twelve-quartered arms by the Royal College of Arms in London about one hundred and fifty years ago.

---

[31] *"Llyfr Baglan",* P. 122.

[32] *"Heraldry and the Herald"* (1982) by Rodney Dennys, P. 66.

[33] *"Ibid.",* P. 64.

[34] Dr. Siddons wrote that the earliest known Welsh motto dates from 1438.

Actually, mottos came into heraldic use at a much later date than arms — first they were in Latin, then French, and lastly English. Whereas the "motto" on the Lewis Coat is surely most appropriate to the historic background of the family of John Lewis the Emigrant to Virginia — it does not appear to be rooted in family records!

At this point in the research it became necessary to change genealogists, for Mr. Twigg wrote that he did not feel himself "competent" to pursue the research into the manuscripts and very early records (going back to medieval times), which was the next step. These records are to be found at the National Library of Wales; so enquiries were made to our friend, Mr. R.W. McDonald, Assistant Keeper of Manuscripts and Records at the National Library at Aberystwyth, asking for a recommendation of a researchist to continue, who fully understood the depth of the research required and the scope of the material to be covered. Mr. McDonald forwarded the name of Dr. Susan J. Davies; in the fall of 1983 she agreed to complete the task of examining *"all"* existing and pertinent records at the Library. She proved to be most capable, well-informed, and entirely dedicated to the work. Dr. Davies teaches *"Palaeography"* at the University — which skill aided her immeasureably in the examination of old inscriptions and Latin manuscripts; at times, she even used an ultra-violet lamp to decipher ancient *"Registers"*. The author is deeply grateful to Dr. Davies for the time, thought, care and effort expended on this pains-taking research, and the author is now certain that nothing exists at the Library which has not been closely examined and evaluated. It would be instructive to list the various records covered by Dr. Davies. They are as follows:

(1) First of all, Dr. Davies ascertained as far as possible which families were identifiable in the area — for elimination purposes.

(2) The most obvious collections of Deeds were covered. Also, the select personal name index and the marriage settlement index.

(3) Civil War events and records were examined for Monmouthshire 1642-1652, as well as Army Lists for any identifiable references to "Lewis."

(4) Examined printed calendars of State Papers, etc., (originals are in London) relating to land forfeiture c. 1650.

(5) Dr. Davies checked on all existing pedigrees.

(6) Sir Joseph Bradney's vast collection of notes for his *"History of Monmouthshire"* is in the National Library at Aberystwyth; Dr. Davies plodded her way through all of them, as well as 47 volumes of "Notes",

including many abstracts of deeds, legal proceedings, etc.; and there are almost the same number of volumes on Monmouthshire *Wills*.

(7) Also perused were a number of important manuscripts concerning the Civil War in the Llangibby Collection at the National Library.

(8) Pertinent *"Parisn Registers"* were read for family notations of baptisms, marriages and deaths — sometimes using an ultra-violet lamp on the old ones.

(9) Covered were numerous indexes of wills — including those which were available at the Library for wills proved at the Prerogative Court of Canterbury; however, there is a gap in the printed indexes after 1639. Bradney's volumes of extracts of wills are very wide-ranging, as he checked Brecon and Llandaff, also London sources.

(10) Lastly, and most productive, Dr. Davies searched the records of the Lordship of Abergavenny, since the Lords of Abergavenny held a great deal of land in that area, in *tenements*.[35]

Under this last group of records Dr. Davies found a really important item. This is the *fact* that there was one JOHN LEWIS listed as holding land in the Town of Abergavenny from the Lord of that place. He was sometimes called a *Merchant*; sometimes, a *Mercer*; sometimes, a *Burgess*.[36] But, most importantly, he was sometimes referred to as a *"Gentleman."* This last appellation was used in that period to denote "arms-bearing." John Lewis occupied 1 1/2 tenements on High Street, which consisted of two houses, with yard and garden that stretched back to the ancient wall of the Town. *Three Rentals* of these tenements were found that dated from *1585, 1627 and 1660.* They were in Latin, heavily abbreviated, so it was most difficult to proceed. The other half of John Lewis' tenement was occupied by one Robert Shershawe, but the whole property had originally belonged to a David Nicholas.

Dr. Davies' "comment" on these facts was most interesting. She wrote: "One might speculate that John Lewis was able to make these purchases after the death of his father." (Lewis Prichard died May 4, 1616.) John Lewis acquired them from one Stephen Hughes, a Vintner (who had

---

[35] *Webster's Dictionary* - *"Law orig.,* that which is subject to tenure; hence land, or any form of incorporeal property treated like land, held by a person of another."

[36] *"History of Monmouthshire"*, Vol. I, Pt. II, P. 153, presents the *"Charter of King Charles I to the Town of Abergavenny,"* November 9, 1638, and named JOHN LEWIS as a Senior Burgess.

obtained them from one David Nicholas) and his wife, Maria, and the payment for the first transaction in September 1616 was for 203 pounds — which Dr. Davies wrote was a great deal of money in those days. Further light was thrown on this evidence by the *Rental of 1627* which included a list of Burgesses in the town with details of their tenements. The most interesting fact is that *there was only "one" John Lewis among the Burgesses,* and in this Rental he was said to live in his *"burgage tenements."*[37] Dr. Davies also wrote that the fact that he was a Mercer — "and prosperous" in a town noted for cloth-making was also interesting. Burgesses often had unusual freedom in the disposal of their property; it was often easier for a Burgess to "sell up and move" than for a landowner to do the same. Abergavenny was hard hit by the commotions of the Civil War; some merchants might very well have preferred to leave. The Rental of 1660 did not include a List of the Burgesses — perhaps, as Dr. Davies wrote, "it had made a tasty lunch for hungry mice!"

In pursuing the matter of "burgage rentals" further, one finds:

"Within the borough the standard unit of land was the *burgage,* the tenure of which gave the holder the privileges and status of a burgess. He was expected to perform a number of duties and obligations to the community as a whole, the most fundamental being centered on the defence of the borough. The burgage plots, which would have fronted that first street, assumed a characteristic shape — long and narrow with a tenement at the front and the remainder used either as a garden or a workshop and yards connected with the particular trade of the tenant. They were almost all let at a fixed, almost standard, rental of one shilling a year. The plots were not uniform in size, varying considerably from town to town and even within towns. The 1/125 sheet of this area shows the burgage plot origins in the lay-out of the properties on the west side of Nevill Street."[38]

In her letter of 26 April, 1984, Dr. Davies writes: "I cannot be precise about all the details of the burgage tenements, because I am working from Bradney's *"Notes"* and extracts of Deeds, so it is not always possible to determine the nature of the transfer of property, eg., whether it is a lease or a purchase. There were two transactions — one in September 1616 and the other in May 1618 — both, I believe were purchases, as

---

[37] *"Random House Dictionary"* (1967), Page 198, *"Burgage"* - Law. Eng., a tenure whereby Burgessess or Townsmen hold lands or tenements of the King or other Lord, usually for a fixed money rent.

[38] *"Medieval Abergavenny"* by GWYN JONES.

substantial amounts of money changed hands. I believe that two adjacent tenements were involved, though this is not entirely clear in the transactions of 1616 and 1618, as they might refer to one and the same property, as the description is not precise. (I know from later evidence that John Lewis had two adjacent properties)."

In Dr. Davies' first Report of 29 January, 1984, she wrote: "I think you have a strong candidate for John Lewis in the baptism of the son of "Lewis Rycketts" in 1591/2 and the marriage of John Lewis Pricket in 1610; also, the deaths of Lewis and Catherine Prichard in 1616 and 1615, respectively." Mr. Twigg had stated that he thought the baptism and the marriage might be of the same person. Then in her second Report of 26 April 1984, she declared: "I have a strong feeling that he *was* the Burgess of Abergavenny." When one considers that Llantilio Pertholey is just one and three-quarters miles down the road from the Town of Abergavenny, certainly the *"place"* is correct; add to that the fact that both *"names"* are identical; finally, as the John Lewis who bought the tenement from Stephen Hughes and Maria his wife in September 1616 must have been *at least* an adult to make such a negotiation (making him born at least by 1595 or before) and as he was the same man who was mentioned in the documents of 1618, 1627 and 1638 — all in the same place of Abergavenny — then, by the *"time"* he would have left Abergavenny for Virginia, he would have been at least fifty-eight years of age. The Emigrant in Virginia died in 1657 (four years later) — supposedly sixty-three years of age. The co-incidences of *Name, Place and Time* — all in agreement — strengthens the old adage of "the authenticity of genealogical facts."

Also, Dr. Davies thought that the Port of Embarkation for the Lewis family would undoubtedly have been Bristol, as that port was close by Wales and was second only to London as a port of departure for the Colonies. Add to that the fact that John Lewis the Burgess, Merchant and Mercer had close mercantile ties with the city of Bristol through Stephen Hughes from whom he purchased his tenement in Abergavenny. Dr. Davies checked with the Records Office in Bristol in an attempt to get information on the departure of the Lewis Family, but, to her chagrin, she discovered that the embarkation records only began in the year 1654 — one year too late!

Dr. Davies did not think that John Lewis was an active participant in the Civil War, as he was too old a man to have fought; but his sympathies were most likely Royalist (considering his background), and she thought that he left Wales primarily because the land he occupied belonged to a Royalist supporter from whom it was probably confiscated by the Parliamentary forces after the defeat of the Royalist effort and the beheading of the king in 1649. Abergavenny had had a strong Royalist loyalty — King Charles I had stayed at "The Priory" (home of James Gunter in Abergavenny) in 1645; and a garrison was maintained at the Castle there which was commanded by Colonel James Proger, the Governor. This latter was of the same family as Johane Lewis, the wife of John Lewis. Sir Charles Somerset was in command of Raglan Castle, and he made an abortive effort to take Abergavenny for the King in 1646.[39]

At this point, it should be noted that during the period of the Civil War and during the Protectorate under Oliver Cromwell immediately afterwards, conditions in Wales, and in Monmouthshire in particular, were in a state of complete upheaval; the Parliamentary forces took over and desecrated the Churches, for they were "Puritans" and the majority of the Churches were "Church of England"; they ravished farms and estates and appropriated whatever they desired; they placed Royalists in jail or under restraint; finally they created chaos with the civil law and judicial system which was left in total disarray — the area being placed in "military districts." This is the principal reason why it is so very difficult to do research in Wales during this period — the records are practically non-existent and we must "make-do" with what is available! However, enough is left to tell the story.

To return to John Lewis the Burgess of Abergavenny! In her third Report of July fourth, Dr. Davies sent some valuable documents to augment the research. She had completed her review of all existing records on this subject at the National Library and had proceeded to contact persons in the Public Record Office in London, the City Archivist at the City of Bristol, and a personal friend in the Gwent County Council. These archivists were kind enough to offer suggestions for future research.

Dr. Davies had copies made of pertinent documents which she sent to me. They are as follows:

(1) *Will of Richard Lewis* of Llangattock, 1627/8 — *Brecon Probate Records 1628/53.*
(2) *Will of Richard Lewis — 1674 — Brecon Probate Records Oct. 1674.*
(3) 10 pages from one volume of Sir Joseph Bradneys *"NOTES"* —Reference — NLW — 7648 D.

---

[39] *"History of Monmouthshire",* Vol. I, Pt. II, page 158.

(4) 2 pages from a *Rental of the Lordship of Abergavenny, 1627*
mentioning John Lewis. Reference — NLW — Abergavenny
Rental No. 2

(5) *Extracts made by her from 2 "Feet of Fines" at the Public Record
Office.* These "Feet of Fines" are with the records of the *Court of
Common Pleas.*

Under the fifth document — "The Fines or Final Concords" — Dr.
Davies goes into detail concerning their meaning. "These are tripartite
agreements in which the purchaser (plaintiff) alleged quite fictitiously
that the person from whom he was buying (the deforciant) had agreed to
convey the property to him but had failed to do so. Before judgment was
given the parties came to a fictitious agreement whereby the vendor
acknowledged that the property really belonged to the purchaser. *One
copy, the foot of fine,* was kept with the records of the Court and it was
secure evidence of title. A fine was a means of conveyance, but fines were
sometimes used for purposes other than simple purchase of property
—they were sometimes used as a means of getting around legal prob-
lems. The reason for "levying-a fine" is often found in a preliminary
document —a *"Covenant".* This, if one can find it, often gives more
information than the fine itself."

NB — (1) Sums of money are often nominal or fictitious.

NB — (2) Several people might join together to levy a fine concerning
various properties not connected with each other.

NB — (3) Acreages, etc., were often approximate.

Dr. Davies was led to some *"fines"* among those for Monmouthshire
at the Public Record Office in London by some references in one of
Bradney's notebooks — he had listed some "fines" for Monmouthshire
for the reign of James I. They were as follows:

(1) *Octaves of Michaelmas 14 James I (6 Oct. 1616)* — before the King's
Justices at Westminster.
   "John Lewis, plaintiff
   Stephen Hughes and Maria his wife, deforciants
   Concerning 1 messuages, 1 curtilage, 2 gardens, with
      appurtenances in Abergavenny.
   SH and M agree that the property belongs to John Lewis,
      and that his heirs shall have it in perpetuity.
   John Lewis gives SH and M 60 pounds."

(2) *Octaves of Michaelmas 15 James I (6 Oct. 1617)* — before the King's Justices at Westminster.

> "Rees (*Riceus* in the Latin original) *Thomas Phillip* and *John Lewis, plaintiffs.*
>
> *Henry Thomas Morgan and Margaret his wife* and *Morgan Thomas ap Thomas and Kathrine his wife* — *deforciants.*
>
> Concerning two messuages, 1 barn, 2 gardens, 1 orchard 20 acres of land, 12 acres of meadow, 10 pasture, and 30 acres of wood, with appurtenances *in Llantilio Pertholey and Aberystouth* (sic.) H and M, M and K, recognize the property/ties to be the right of Rees, as those which Rees and John received from H and M, M and K. It is recognized that the properties shall be held by Rees and John and the heirs of Rees, in perpetuity. Rees and John gave H and M, M and K 60 pounds."

NB — From Dr. Davies: "Number 2 is probably an example of two people joining together for convenience in levying a "Fine" concerning separate properties, obviously with slightly different terms. Unfortunately we are not told which of the plaintiffs has acquired the property! (sic) So this is not a great deal of help, *apart from providing a probable link with a John Lewis and Llantilio Pertholey in 1617.*"

Dr. Davies continues in her Report of July 4th: "The 'Final Concords' from the Public Record Office are interesting in this context. The one indicates that a John Lewis may have acquired property in Llantilio Pertholey in 1617. I am certain that the other refers to his acquisition of burgage tenements in Abergavenny, as related on the pages from Bradney's 'Notes.' "

However, upon more extensive research on this matter of the "Fine" of Oct. 6, 1617, additional information came to light which proved to be of inestimable value to the research. The "Fine" dealt with a Law Suit brought by one *Rees Thomas Philip* and one *John Lewis* — of Aberystoth (sic) and Llantilio Pertholey, respectively — "Plaintiffs" — against two members of the *Morgan Family* as "Deforciants" (*Deforciant* — in the *"Random House Dictionary"*, copyrighted, 1966, 1967, page 379, it gives the following interpretation: "Law —to withhold-property, especially land — by force or violence, as from the rightful owner)." The Suit was before the King's Justices at Westminster and the verdict was in favour of the Plaintiffs. According to Dr. Davies it reads: "It is recognized that the property shall be held by Rees and John and the heirs of Rees in perpetuity." Rees and John gave the Morgan Family sixty pounds in money to seal it.

According to the patronymics system of Wales, the *Rees Thomas Philip* who is quoted in the "Fine" with John Lewis as "Plaintiff" is undoubtedly the son of *Thomas Philip Llewellyn of Llanelly, Llangattuck-Nigh-Uske, Brecknockshire,* who is mentioned in the Bradney's Pedigree of the Lewis of Llanelly Family (Rhys Goch Line).[40] This Thomas Philip Llewellyn is named as the father of *NEST* — the wife of Richard Lewis, Senior, Gent., of Liangattuck, Crickhowell, in the pedigree, whose WILL of 1628 has been cited (mentioning his children and grandchildren) and who was the father of *LEWIS RYCKETTS (RICHARDS)* who died in Llantilio Pertholey on May 4, 1616, leaving *Thomas, Maudelen and John Lewis.*

Also, there is another reference which states:[41] *"Thomas Philip Llewellyn married Margaret, the daughter of John G'll'm Thomas of Llangeneder, one of the patrons there, who descended paternalie of Kynyllin ap Rees Goch."* (Kynyllin is another form of Genillin — who was the son of Rhys Goch and the ancestor from whom John Lewis traced his origin). All these persons including John Lewis, bore the Arms of Rhys Goch, and on the maternal side they went back to Llangeneder. This last-mentioned fact verifies in still another manner the origin of the *Rhys Goch Arms* from Llewellyn ap Ynyr of Ial (or Yale) in Denbighshire — to whom they were granted in 1256 by Gruffydd ap Madoc, Prince of Dinas Bran, for extreme valour in battle.[42]

As Llantilio Pertholey was undoubtedly the property of John Lewis, then the other property involved must have been that of Rees Thomas Philip in Aberystouth. The author has identified this property as being located in the *Parish of Aberystruth.* In an "antiquarian" book purchased in Abergavenny entitled: *"The Illustrated History and Biography of Brecknockshire from the Earliest Times to the Present Day",* by Edwin Poole, published in 1886, one finds on page 235 of same, under the *"Town of Brynmawr", under the Parish of Llanelly,* the following: "Brynmawr (Big Mountain), anciently called Wain-elygan (Willow Tree Common) on the confines of Breckonshire, where the parishes of Llangynider, Llanelly, and Llangattuck of Brecknockshire and Aberystruth of Monmouthshire meet . . . in the Hundred and Union of Crickhowell and Tredegar, southern division of the rural Deanery of Crickhowell

---

[40] *"History of Monmouthshire",* Vol. I, Pt. II, P. 339.

[41] *"Llyfr Baglan",* Page 47.

[42] *"Heraldic Visitation of Wales",* Vol. II, Page 232; also, *"The Llyfr Baglan",* Page 111 and 47.

(third Part); archdeanery of Brecknock." This *Aberystruth* is most probably the location of the second property of the "Fine" of 1617 — and once more it would tie together John Lewis of Llantilio Pertholey Parish and Rees Thomas Philip of Aberystruth Parish — both linked to Brecknockshire by *Thomas Philip Llewellyn of Llanelly Parish* — who was father to *NEST* (grandmother of John Lewis) and to *REES THOMAS PHILIP of Aberystruth*. Rees would have been great-uncle to John Lewis; and Aberystruth would have been "land" in the neighborhood of Rees' grandmother, Margaret — daughter of the patron of Llangeneder. We have a saying in Virginia Genealogy — *"When one finds the Land, one finds the Blood."*

The estate in Llantilio Pertholey which was confirmed to John Lewis by the Justices at Westminster in 1617 was most likely that of "Ty-Hir", with an approximate acreage of 72 acres, according to the "Fine" description of that date. This estate is at the farthest, southern end of the Parish, at the foothills of the mountain. When John Lewis decided to emigrate to Virginia, this property went into the possession of the family of Shershawe of Abergavenny. One Robert Shershawe was the next-door neighbor and occupant of 1/2 of John Lewis' "Burgage tenement" in that city. There is apparently no record of the transfer of this estate from John Lewis, as many records of this period are missing, due to the unsettled conditions of the "Protectorate". However, in the WILL of Miss Elizabeth Shershawe, Spinster, of Abergavenny,[43] 1680, this property went into the hands of several of her nieces and nephews, and after changes over a number of years, it finally was sold by a *Trust* to the descendants of the elder line of Richard Lewis, Senior, of Crickhowell Llangattuck, Brecknockshire. It is no longer in the family of Lewis, but the author consulted with Mr. Watkins of Wern-ddu, whose wife was a close friend of the wife of the last Lewis owner of "Ty-Hir," and he verified the acreage of the estate as being practically identical with that described in the "Fine" of 1617. It is a very old house of native stone — called even now "Ty-Hir" — which means "Long House." The family must have continued to reside there, at least partially, prior to John Lewis' leaving for Virginia, as the record of his last son (from whom the Gloucester County, Virginia, line claims descent) was noted in the *"Register"* of Saint Teilo was *"John son of John Lewis baptized December 15, 1633."*

---

[43] Bradney's *"History of Monmouthshire"*, Vol. I, Pt. II, Pages 288 and 289.

"Ty-Hir", being situated in the Parish of Llantilio Pertholey, was definitly Morgan (Herbert) land —that family being lords of the Manor of "Triley," most recently Watkin Morgan, Gent., who was also Lord of Pen-y-Clawdd in Llanfihangel Crucorney. The land of Watkin Morgan was in Llantilio Pertholey —on the slope of the Deri Mountain; and naturally, *his* land in that Parish would have descended to his children and grandchildren — such as Catherine (wife of Lewis Prichard) his daughter, and John Lewis, his grandchild.

One last matter remains concerning the "Fine" of 1617, and that is an identification of the *"Morgan Family"* who were the "deforciants" in the Law Suit of Rees Thomas Philip and John Lewis. They must, of necessity, have had a claim to the land, very likely from inheritance, as at that period most transfers of land were by right of inheritance. After much searching through authoritative sources the author located a pedigree of the Morgan Family of Llanwenarth Parish.[44] This is a family who bore the same Coat-of-Arms as John Lewis of Llantilio Pertholey. A note of Mr. Bradney'[45] states that Mr. Theophilus Jones (the recognized authority on Brecknockshire) made an error in regard to the pedigree of this Morgan of Llanwenarth family, giving them the Coat of HERBERT, when in fact they were descended from the *"Ynyr Gwent" Line* (their paternal descent), although they apparently assumed the Coat of Rhys Goch — probably through an heiress from that family.

In the pedigree in Bradney are listed the two names mentioned in the "Fine" of 1617 — *"Harry (Henry) ap Thomas and Morgan ap Thomas"* who were sons of *Thomas ap Morgan (living in 1568) and Gwenllian, daughter of David ap Gruffydd ap Thomas Coly of Llanwenarth, heiress to lands in Llanfihangel Crucorney; married before 1568."* This Thomas Morgan had as his heir one *John ap Thomas Morgan of Llanwenarth Gent.*, who was a plaintiff in a *Chancery Suit dated June 26, 1588.*[46] His obituary was dated 2 April 1619, and his WILL was dated 15 June 1610 and proved 30 April 1611 (P.C.C. Wood 34). His wife, *Gwenllian*, was another child of *Thomas Philip Llewellyn of Llanelly*; she dated her WILL 17 Feb. 1625 and it was proved 22 Nov. 1626 (P.C.C. Hele, 121). She was "sister" to Rhys Thomas Philip and "Great-Aunt" to John Lewis of Llantilio Pertholey. The two of the Morgan Family named as deforciants in the "Fine" of 1617 were younger brothers of this John ap Thomas Morgan who had the Chancery Suit.

---

[44] Bradney's *"History of Monmouthshire"*, Vol. I, Pt. II, Page 352.
[45] *"History of Monmouthshire"*, Vol. I, Pt. II, P. 351.
[46] *Chancery Proceedings*, Eliz. T.t, 20.

The mother of John ap Thomas Morgan, wife of Thomas ap Morgan, was an heiress to lands in Llanfihangel Crucorney on the side of her mother, who, was undoubtedly a daughter of Watkin Morgan, Gent., of Pen-y-clawdd; hence, on her father's side she would have carried the blood of this Morgan (HERBERT) line into the family of Llanwenarth — so perhaps Mr. Theophilus Jones was not entirely incorrect when he called them "Herberts." Later members of this family intermarried with the Lewis of Ysgyrid line of which John Lewis' wife, Johane, was a daughter. These inter-relationships are given to point up the fact of the "blood" connections between these people involved in the "Fine" of 1617 and the right of *all* of them to lands in Llanfihangel Crucorney. This was land owned by the POWELL (ap Howell) family of the "de Bredwarden Line", who had inter-married with the sole heiress of the Manor of Pen-y-Clawdd in Llanfihangel Crucorney, and *jure ux.*, had become Lord of the Manor. It had come to them from a daughter and sole heir of Ralph ap Sitsyllt (Cecil) and had previously been a part of the Lordship of Abergavenny. The de Bredwarden family were descended from a Norman Knight who came to Wales with Bernard de Newmarsh after the Norman Conquest, who became Earl of Hereford; a great-grandson, Sir Roger de Bredwarden, was awarded the Manor of Gwernvale in Brecknockshire, and the family lived for quite a number of generations in close proximity to the Lewis of Llanelly family of Llangattuck.

This "Fine" of 1617 is so important because it traces the pedigree of the families by means of tenure of land — which is always the best genealogical source. The "Common Denominator" of those persons mentioned in the "Fine" is the *POWELL FAMILY*, and the land involved is that in Llanfihangel Crucorney. That is the land which Gwenllian Powell brought to Watkin Morgan, Gent., on marriage. The land in Llantilio Pertholey mentioned in the "Fine" of 1617 was undoubtedly land inherited from Watkin Morgan of Pen-y-Clawdd which had been *his* before marriage, as *"Lord of Triley."* However, the two pieces of land — in Llantilio Pertholey and Llanfihangel Crucorney — tie together the pedigrees of all these people — as all were of the Powell blood and of the Morgan (Herbert) blood of Llantilio Pertholey.

The *Coly Family of Llanwenarth* from whom the Morgans of that Parish obtained their claim to the lands in Llanfihangel Crucorney are traced under the title of *"Cummerre"* (Cymerau)[47] which is located in Llantilio Crosseny Parish where the Powell family were settled for some

---

[47] *"Llyfr Baglan"*, pages 144 and 145.

time. In fact, the Coly Family had inter-married with the Powells for several generations so they were often "cousins," as were most of the nobility and gentry of Wales at that period! There is an *Indenture*[48] dated 31 July, 1603, concerning a post-nuptial settlement of the Morgan Family which names *"our well-beloved in Christ, Richard Lewis of Llangattuck, Gent."* (grandfather to John Lewis) and *"Valentine Prichard"* of Llanddewi Ysgyrid (step-father to Johane Lewis, wife of John Lewis), indicating the close relationships involved. All three of the families mentioned in the "Fine" of 1617 in Llantilio Pertholey were related by ties of blood and had inherited claims to the land in question through their antecedents. The fact that "Ty-Hir" was awarded to John Lewis by the Justices at Westminster would appear to mean that *his* claim to the estate was stronger than that of the Morgan Family of Llanwenarth —perhaps he was descended from an elder child of Watkin Morgan, Gent., and Gwenllian Powell, or perhaps the estate had been promised to his mother, Catherine Richard (Prichard) by her parents.

Aside from the "Final Concords", the research pages from Bradney's *"Notes"* which Dr. Davies sent in her "Report", provided several new thoughts. The top entry on *page 28* of same dealt with the transfer of property to one *Thomas Lewis,* dated 25 Jan. 1655 — just two years after John Lewis emigrated to Virginia! The description of the property involved appears to be identical with that of the "burgage tenement" which the latter had occupied in Abergavenny for years — on High Street. This Thomas Lewis could very well be the older brother of John Lewis who was mentioned in the WILL of the grandfather, Richard Lewis (1628). He would be taking over the property when John Lewis went to Virginia.

However, the most important item from these *"Notes"* of Bradney on page 66 of same was a "DEED OF FFEEOFFMENT," dated May 6, 1652 (six months before John Lewis left the country of Wales for Virginia). It was between one *JOHN PREES (Price) of the Parish of Old Castle Yeoman and Margaret his wife of the one part and James Davies of the Parish of Llanfihangel Crucorney Yeoman of the other part.* This sale included 2 messages and 2 closes and it was described as being located in Llanfihangel Crucorney. The bounds are mentioned as being "from Penbiddle towards Campston." But the most important part of the DEED was the fact that these lands were *"lately purchased by them from John Lewis and others."* The date of the DEED, May 6, 1652, was

---

[48] *"History of Monmouthshire",* Vol. I, Pt. II, page 351.

the first indication that John Lewis was selling his property just prior to leaving for Virginia. Allowing some time for the sale of the property, the arrangements for the voyage to America, the actual trip, and the waiting period for the House of Burgesses to award him the Grant of Land for his Headrights, this is about as close as one could come to the date of July 1, 1653, when his Grant of Land shows he is resident in Virginia.. The last four words of the phrase — "John Lewis and others" — would indicate that they had acquired this piece of land from an inherited estate. It would also appear that John Lewis' wife was not alive at this point, or she surely would have been mentioned, as were the wives of the Grantor and Grantee in the DEED (This was the customary procedure in law at that time, as wives always had a "dower" interest in property).

The next step was to research the various owners of the land in this area of Llanfihangel Crucorney. The chief estate of "Penbiddle" (described in the Deed) was *"Upper Penbiddle"*.[49] This was a hamlet in the Hundred of Skenfrith and the Manor of Grossmont or Llangua. There were three farms — the old farmhouse on the north side of the road is still standing, much in its original state. This is the identical property which was purchased from John Price of Old Castle (who had bought it of John Lewis and others) *in 1652* by James Davies. This land is definitely that of the outstanding family of *Powell* — in fact, in earlier times, one Walter Powell is spoken of as *"Lord of the Manor of Penbiddle."*[50]

Under the Hundred of Skenfrith[51] is an account of "Llantilio Court." It is the principal seat of the Parish, a large estate being annexed to it. It was the home of one Walter Powell (called "of Llanarth") who was the son of Thomas Powell (ap Howell) of Penhros, great-nephew to Gwenllian Powell who was married to Watkin Morgan, Gent., of "Triley" in Llantilio Pertholey Parish. Walter Powell moved to Llantilio Court, the outstanding "seat" in Llantilio Crosseny Parish, in the early part of the seventeenth century — before that he had resided "at Llanarth". He was a staunch Royalist who suffered greatly at the hands of the Parliamentary Party. He was also Deputy-Steward and Receiver of Rents to the Earl of Worcester. He appears to have been a well-educated, responsible and meticulous man. He wrote a *"Diary"* of his life which has been published (covering his life up to July 1, 1655) and edited by Sir Joseph Bradney

---

49 "*History of Monmouthshire*", Vol. I, Pt. II, pages 224 and 225.
50 "*The Llyfr Baglan*", by John Williams, edited by Bradney, pages 63 and 63 n.
51 "*History of Monmouthshire*", Vol. I, Pt. I, page 94.

(1906), an introduction including the *WILL of WALTER POWELL*,[52] dated 29 December, 1655, and proved 11 Oct., 1656 (P.C.C. Berkeley 349). In this Will Walter Powell calls one Walter Morgan — *"my cousin"*. A little further on in the Will, he states: *"Whereas I hold two leases from Walter Morgan and William Morgan of Llantilio Pertholey."* Thus, *Walter Powell's contemporary, Walter Morgan of Llantilio Pertholey Parish, was his "cousin."* The author is aware that the term "cousin" was often taken "loosely" in former time, but it has always denoted a "blood relationship." Moreover, the William Morgan of Llantilio Pertholey Parish also mentioned by Walter Powell was the heir of Watkin Morgan, Gent., Lord of Pen-y-Clawdd. William Morgan left as his heir *only* a grand-daughter.

Now the Walter Morgan of Llantilio Pertholey Parish (who was cousin to Walter Powell of Llanarth) was the son of one *Charles Morgan, Gent.,* of the same parish, whose ob. was 11 Dec. 1636 and whose inq. p.m. was 27 Sept. 1637.[53] In the resumé of Charles Morgan his son is listed as Walter Morgan, esq., who lived at "Ty-Mawr" in the same parish, aet. 30 in 1637. This is the identical Walter Morgan mentioned in the Will of Walter Powell as his *cousin.*

At this point, the author would, with due respect, take exception to Mr. Bradney's interpretation of Charles Morgan as *"probably"* the son of William Morgan of Arxton (Hereford). While the latter is on the same *Morgan Pedigree*-[54] of the line of The Chapel in Abergavenny, Llanfihangel Crucorney, Triley and Pen-y-Clawdd, who bore Arms "per pale azure and gules, three lions rampant argent," it is much more likely that Charles Morgan was a younger son to Watkin Morgan, Gent., as the land of Charles Morgan was in Llantilio Pertholey and was later held by his son Walter Morgan; that property would have descended to him from Charles Morgan's father whose land was "of Triley."

There appears to be a definite connection between the family of Charles Morgan, Esq., and John Lewis — both of Llantilio Pertholey Parish and both inheriting and holding land in *Penbiddle, Llanfihangel Crucorney.* Charles Morgan's estate was called *"Upper Stanton"* and John Lewis' was called *"Upper Penbiddle."*

Now, if, as it appears, these Morgans and Lewises intermarried with

---

[52] *"The Diary of Walter Powell"*, edited by Bradney in 1906, page viii of the Introduction.

[53] *"The History of Monmouthshire"* (Bradney), Vol. I, Pt. II, page 203.

[54] *"The History of Monmouthshire"* (Bradney), Vol. I, Pt. II, page 218.

the Powell line, they would have had every right to share in the lands of that family in Llanfihangel Crucorney. Gwenllian Powell, wife of Watkin Morgan, Gent., was the daughter of *Rawlin ap Watkin fychan, jure ux.* Lord of Pen-y-Clawdd; her mother was the daughter and sole heiress of *Ralph ap Sitsyllt, Lord of Pen-y-Clawdd.* Reiterating, before that generation the family had resided at Crickhowell, Brecon, where the ancestor, one Roger de Bredwarden, great-grandson of Sir Walter de Bredwarden, Earl of Hereford, was granted the Manor of Gwernvale by Sir Hugh de Turberville for Knight's service, in the time of Edward I. This family lived in close proximity to the Lewis of Llanelly family of Llangattuck. After intermarriage with the Sitsyllt family, they went to Llanfihangel Crucorney for three generations, and then Walter Powell of Llanarth leased the estate of Llantilio Court in Llantilio Crosseny.

To further strengthen the connection between the families and the land they inherited, the author wishes to quote from Bradney again —[55] which reads: "LLwyn-ffranc (Frank's Grove) belonged in the seventeenth century to Charles Morgan of Llantilio Pertholey, who at his death, November 11, 1636, was seized of the estate. His son Walter Morgan, possessed the two farms of Llwyn-ffranc, which, with other property he settled on his son James on his marriage in 1665." This is the identical area of Penbiddle mentioned in Bradney's *"Notes"* — in the *Deed of Ffeoffment* when John Price sold land in Penbiddle to James Davies —land which he had recently in 1652 bought *"from John Lewis and others."* The family of Davies was the recipient of the land in both cases. The other lands in the hamlet were later sold in 1682 by William Herbert of Llangattuck, esq., who had earlier purchased them from John Parry, of Llanfihangel Crucorney, esq. This same *John Parry* was Lord of Pen-y-Clawd and was mentioned as of this place in a pre-nuptial settlement of David Morgan of Llanwenarth in an Indenture of 20 Jan, 1644.[56]

At this point the author wishes to state that she always thought there was a connection between John Lewis of Llantilio Pertholey and Watkin Morgan, Gent., of "Triley" and his wife Gwenllian Powell (ap Howell), for John Lewis named his first child *"Gwenllian"*, his second child *"Lettus"* (Lettyce), and his third child *"Watkin."* These were all names in the Powell-Morgan Family, and not at all to be found in the Rhys Goch Line from whom Lewis Prichard descended. If all the deductions prove

---

[55] *"The History of Monmouthshire"* (Bradney), Vol. I, Pt. II, page 217.
[56] *"Ibid.",* page 351.

correct, then John Lewis would have inhertited the land in Llanfihangel Crucorney from his mother, Catherine Morgan, daughter of Watkin Morgan, Gent., and Gwenllian Powell. *"Watkin Morgan, Gent."* was buried on March 18, 1592/3 (page 2 of the *"Register"* of St. Teilo's; a *Gwenllian Howell* was buried at the same Church on July 24, 1596 (page 4 of the *"Register")*.*Mr. Twigg had stated that it was the custom of that period for married ladies to keep their maiden names. *Catherine Richard (Prichard)* was buried at St. Teilo's on Sept. 29, 1615, and her husband *Lewis Prichard* was buried at the same Church on May 4, 1616. The *"Register"* of St. Teilo's does not begin until 1591, so there is no record of the births or marriage of these persons, but their genealogical descent has been defined "through the land." The land in Penbiddle, Llanfihangel Crucorney, with its inheritance by Charles Morgan and John Lewis, is clear evidence of blood relationship; and the author feels confident that Charles Morgan and Catherine Morgan (wife of Lewis Prichard) were brother and sister; and that their children — Walter Morgan and John Lewis — were "cousins," — together with Walter Powell of Llanarth. Evidently, John Lewis did not want to part with his inheritance, but necessity demanded when he prepared to journey to Virginia. "The others" involved with him in the Deed could possibly be his brother "Thomas" and his sister "Maudelen", as noted in the WILL of his grandfather, Richard Lewis of Brecon (1628).

The author is deeply indebted to Dr. Davies for her pains-taking plodding through the volumes of *"Notes"* of Sir Joseph Bradney at the National Library of Wales at Aberystywyth, searching for *every* mention of the name of LEWIS; for, without having found the DEED of John Price to James Davies in 1652, and mention of his *having purchased it lately from John Lewis and others,* there would have been no "clue" to lead to the connection with the Powell Family of Llanfihangel Crucorney and Llantilio Crosseny — and the mother of John Lewis of Llantilio Pertholey! Dr. Davies is a fine researchist — a perfectionist.

Before leaving the subject of the land and old homes of the Family in this area, there are several other homes connected with the families of John Lewis in Gwent (Monmouthshire). The most interesting is *Wernddu-* the oldest extant home in the county. It is the seat of the Senior Line of the HERBERT FAMILY, who until recently bore the name of PROGER. Members of this family were very prominent in the time of the Stuarts — several being "Gentlemen of the Bedchamber" to those monarchs. Wern-ddu is still a lovely home, due to the care and vision of the Watkins family who now own it. It has been beautifully restored and the gardens are a sight to behold in full bloom! There is, near the front entrance, a most interesting old "Staircase" of great age. The present owners told the author about a Catholic Chapel in the Attic of the home, used during the period of the establishment of the Anglican State Religion in Wales — for the Progers remained Catholic to the end! It is highly likely that Elizabeth Proger of Wern-ddu, second wife to William Lewis of Llanddewi Ysgyrid, was baptized in this Attic Chapel, as well as her daughter, Johane, wife to John Lewis. One has a feeling of antiquity and continuity upon entering and viewing this delightful home, for it has been lovingly restored by the family of *Watkins, the head of whom is a Herbert of Wern-ddu.*

Then there is *Pen-y-Clawdd"* which had originally belonged to the Lords of Abergavenny, but had gone into the hands of a branch of the Sitsyllt (Cecil) family. It is a most impressive mansion of native stone, a fine example of Elizabethan architecture, and it was added on to during several generations. The name means "head of the dyke" and it is standing close to an earthwork surrounded by two moats. One has a definite feeling of great antiquity and history upon viewing this site. It has recently been sold by the last member of the GABB family who have owned it for a long time. This is the home from which Gwenllian Powell married Watkin Morgan, Gent., of "Triley."

And, lastly, there is the *Manor of "Triley,"* which has been broken up into a number of farms and no longer exists as such. It was sometimes called *"Tre-lech (Stone Town)"* (on the slope of the Deri Mountain) —later called *"Arcadia."* It encompassed several farms and estates, and had belonged to the Morgan (Herbert) Family who had been previously seated at The Chapel and Llanfihangel Crucorney. One of the later homes, known as *"Triley Court"* has been made into a lovely nursing home for the elderly; it was originally a hunting lodge of the Morgan family. "Ty-Hir" was a part of the Herbert of Llantilio Pertholey land.

At this point the author would like to go into another field of research accomplished by Dr. Davies. On her own initiative she pursued the other names mentioned in the WILL of Richard Lewis of Brecon (1628). She found among the *Brecon WILLS* "Letters of administration for *EDWARD PRICHARD, LLANELLI, CO.BRECON, GENT., 1635."* There is no Will for this gentleman; he died intestate. His wife was one Gwenllian James, and there is a bond in her name and that of a James Lewis, Gent. *(Note of Dr. Davies —* "A James Lewis was cousin to Richard Lewis, Junior"¹). The appraisers of Edward Prichard's goods and chattels were *John Prichard* and *Thomas Meredith.* This Edward Prichard is no doubt the Uncle of John Lewis — who was Executor of his own father's WILL in 1628 and guardian of the young Richard, the heir.

33

He is from the identical parish (Llanelli) of the Lewis family of Brecon. Also Dr. Davies found a WILL for one *THOMAS PRICHARD OF LLANGATTUCK CO. BRECON.,* proved in 1635. He had a number of sons, including *William Thomas* and *John Thomas* and several daughters. Among the witnesses to Thomas Prichard's Will were *William Prichard* and *John Meredith.* A John Meredith was one of the appraisers of the goods of Richard Lewis (1628). Moreover, one daughter of Richard Lewis, the younger, married a *Roger Meredith,* and this Richard had bought lands from an *Edward John Meredith* of Llangattuck. This Thomas Prichard Will is without doubt that of the other Uncle of John Lewis who is mentioned in the grandfather's WILL.

The only other son of Richard Lewis of 1628 who has not been identified is that of his "heir" — or so called by the authoritative *"History of Brecknock"*[57] of that area. This genealogy is also reiterated by Mr. Peter C. Bartrum[58] in his newest publication which has just been recently published by the National Library of Wales. Considering such eminent authorities, I believe we can accept the fact that Richard Lewis of Llangattuck had as his "heir", or eldest son, one *William Lewis.* Theophilus Jones continues the information a little further and states that William Lewis held a degree of LLB. (Doctor of Law).

If this is true, then this son (the heir) would have most likely been educated in England, either at Oxford or Cambridge Universities and the first of the sons of Richard Lewis to assume the name of Lewis. A perusal of a list of students of both of these colleges resulted in only three names listed as William Lewis. There were none at Cambridge, but at Oxford,[59] were found:

(1) William Lewis of Monmouthshire, gent: Magdelen College; matriculated 1561, aged 18.
(2) William Lewis of Monmouthshire, gent.: New Hall Inn; matriculated 1586 aged 16.
(3) William Lewis: BA St. Mary Hall, 1586/7; M.A. Gloucester Hall 1592/3; B.C.L. 1596.[60]

Of these three men the only one to obtain a Law Degree was the last. If he received his first Degree of B.A. in 1586/7 then he probably matricu-

---

[57] *"History of Brecknock"* by Theophilus Jones (1909).
[58] "Pedigree of Rhys Goch of Ystrad-Yw," page 1544 of the latest *"Genealogy"* by Mr. Peter C. Bartrum.
[59] *"Alumni Oxoniesis"*
[60] *"B.C.L."* - Degree of Bachelor of Civil Law.

lated at least three years earlier — or in 1583. Mr. Twigg wrote: "If we accept one of these three men as relating to William Lewis, the son of Richard (Will 1628), we have his date of birth as around 1563 or 1570, and this sort of dating would very well fit the third candidate also." Judging from what Mr. Twigg wrote, one would expect to locate a William Lewis born about 1563. This would make his brother Lewis Prichard born a few years later, about 1565.

It appears valid that the third William Lewis listed at Oxford was educated as an Attorney-at-Law. Among the *"Notes* of Bradney which Dr. Davies reviewed, she sent the author an excerpt on page 20 of same — it is a transfer of property on High Street in Abergavenny to John Lewis from Stephen Hughes on September 6, 1616, and included in the DEED is the statement that Stephen Hughes *"appointed his loving friends, William Lewys and Lewys James, Gent., his attorneys."* This William Lewys (Lewis) could very well be the elder brother of Lewis Prichard (of Llantilio Pertholey Parish), Edward Prichard and Thomas Prichard! Mr. Twigg wrote that if William Lewis were well-fixed in life and a successful attorney, then Richard Lewis the elder could possibly have left the estate at Llangattuck to William's son — for surely, an attorney would have little use for an estate in the country! If this is the elder brother of Lewis Prichard, then he was alive in 1616. There is always the possibility that he was deceased by 1628 when his father wrote his WILL.

And now we come to an extremely important part of the research. The Will of Richard Lewis the elder in 1628 especially names all his children *except William*; they have all been identified to date. However, Richard Senior names "Richard" a young boy as his heir — for whom there is no other explanation except that he is the son of William Lewis. Also, he wills "to Elizabeth Lewis, daughter." This was a puzzle to Mr. Twigg, but now it comes into position; for this *Elizabeth Lewis* is undoubtedly the widow of Richard's eldest son William; and the three grand-daughters mentioned together as *"Marie, Elizabeth and Doritie"* were most likely her own, together with the son *Richard*. The author gives as substantiating evidence of these relationships a Pedigree from *"The Llyfr Baglan"*. This pedigree is one of the family of *MORGAN OF MACHEN*,[61] *and it definitely states that one daughter, "Elizabeth married William Lewis of Abergavenny."* This entry is in the position of the last generation of that family, and as the *"Llyfr Baglan"* was compiled

---

[61] *"The Llyfr Baglan"*, pages 175 and 176.

between the years 1600 and 1607, it falls within the "time" frame. Elizabeth Morgan was the daughter of Thomas Morgan, esq., of Tretegire, who married Elizabeth, daughter of Roger Bodenham, esq., of Rothoros. Her brother was Sir William Morgan of Tredeger, Knight. This is further strengthened by the fact that Richard Lewis, Junior, in his WILL of 1674 called *William Morgan "cousin german"*.[62] So, it would appear that William Lewis, LLB., was deceased between 1616 and 1628. However, it appears probable that he *was* the attorney of Abergavenny and the husband of *Elizabeth Morgan* and the father of *Richard, Marie, Elizabeth* and *Doritie* (all grandchildren of Richard Lewis, Senior, and mentioned in his WILL of 1628). This brings to a conclusion the identification of almost all of the immediate family of Richard Lewis of Llangattuck. The final step is to trace the historical background of this family in Wales and to set forth its record in Virginia!

First, the author wishes to deal with the lineage in Wales, quoting from the Heraldic authority of Wales, the former Herald Extraordinary, Major Francis Jones: *"The Theory of Welsh Gentility."*[63] In Wales there was no such thing as 'the armigerous gentlemen.' The theory was, that a man was gentle by virtue of his genealogy. Gentility followed blood. This concept of biological aristocracy had deep roots. and it continued to be asserted even as late as the nineteenth century. It is of particular importance to note that the English Heralds of Tudor or later times recognized this evaluation of gentility in relations to Welsh armorial claims."

And further on, under the title of *"The Heraldic Ancestor"*,[64] Major Jones continues: "The bards decreed that all the royal and tribal ancestors should be given coats-of-arms . . . where a family bore arms, the bards stated that, in reality, these had been inherited from a tribal ancestor, and accordingly assigned them to that ancestor . . . It was asserted that since a Welshman derived his gentility from ancestors, he was entitled also to derive from them his arms, real or assigned . . . Accordingly, Welsh heraldry acquired a dual purpose. In England a coat-of-arms was often entirely divorced from ancestry; in Wales, *it was the result of ancestry.* The Welsh coat-of-arms is not merely a mark of gentility — it is the portrait of an ancestor, as vivid as the canvas of a Goya, or Vandyke, or Graham Sutherland."

---

[62] *"Cousin German"* - *"Cousin of the Blood."*
[63] "The Coat-of-Arms" by Major Francis Jones, Vol. V, pages 350 and 351.
[64] *"Ibid.",* Vol. V, page 351.

The line of Rhys Goch is an illustrious one! There are fourteen generations of the family from the Emigrant ancestor to the present adult generation in Virginia. There are fourteen generations from JOHN LEWIS (born in Monmouthshire in 1591/92) back to RHYS GOCH ("the red-haired"), Lord of Ystrad-Yw and Ewyas.[65] There are fourteen more generations back from Maenyrch (father of Rhys Goch) back to Caradawg Freichfras, ("the brawny-armed"), Knight of King Arthur's Round Table;[66] and lastly, there are five more generations back from Caradawg to Coel Godeborg, "ancient King of Britain"[67] — going back approximately to 385 A.D. In all, there are forty-seven generations of this line — documented as well as it is possible to do so — back into the mists of Welsh History and Genealogy. It is a most unusal genealogy, and it would not have been possible if it were not for the "unique" system of Bards which the Celtic people originated.

Although Lewis Rycketts (Prichard), son of Richard Lewis of Llangattuck married into Monmouthshire and died there, it might be useful at this point to describe in some detail the land which had been the home of this family of LEWIS for centuries, Brecknockshire, named for its first great Welsh ruler, BRYCHAN. It is an inland county of Wales, the fourth largest, bounded on the northwest by Cardigan, on the north and northeast by Radnor, on the east and southeast by Monmouthshire, on the south by Glamorgan, and on the west by Carmarthen. It is almost entirely encircled by mountains, except for the Vale of the Usk River at Crickhowell. The Usk and the Wye "valleys" became the "ways" through the mountains for the English. The conquest of the district by the Romans was about 75-80 A.D.; they established small forts throughout the territory to maintain control. With the departure of the Romans the hill tribes gained possession of the area under the celebrated BRYCHAN — his land lying wholly east of the Eppynt Range. Brychan gave his name to the county, and most of the older churches of central Brecknockshire were founded by, or dedicated to, members of Brychan's family. He became the ancestor of one of the three chief tribes of hereditary Welsh saints. His seventeenth daughter, GWEN, married Llyr Morini and they became the parents of Caradawg Freichfras, legendary Knight of the Round Table, "cousin" to King Arthur, who obtained the territory of Brecknockshire for his subsequent heirs from his mother *Gwen.*

---

[65] "The History of Monmouthshire", Bradney, pages 338 and 339.
[66] *"Llyfr Baglan",* Pp. 94, 94n, 120.
[67] *"Ibid.",* P. 120.

The Welsh rose to their greatest heights under the banner of King Arthur. Caradawg was one of his three great Cavalry leaders and his "Chief Councelor." After the glory of the defeat of the Angles and Saxons, came a period of "dark ages" during which the land was still ruled by Welsh chieftains and princelings.

When the Normans came in the last quarter of the eleventh century, Bernard de Newmarsh defeated the last of the Welsh rulers of Brecknockshire — Bleddyn ap Maenyrch, brother to Rhys Goch, died at "Battle" in 1090. Bernard established himself at Brecon, where he built a strong castle; he made Brecon his *"Caput de Baroniae;"* however, he also created the important monastic house of the Priory of St. John the Baptist; there was also the Dominican friary established to the southwest of Brecon, which was refunded by Henry VIII in 1542 as a collegiate church and school; this institution is now known as Christ's College.

Brecon has always been important in the trade of Wales — principally for wool and leather, and there were several fairs for the promotion of this. The Guild Hall at Brecon was the seat of the various Guilds of the county. The weavers, inspired by the refugees from the Continent, became quite prominent there. Politically, ecclesiastically and culturally — the county of Brecknock has always been of great importance to the British Isles.

The family of LEWIS OF LLANELLY is widely written up in *"A History of Brecknockshire"*[68] by Theophilus Jones. He states that it was the Cadet Branch of the line of Rhys Goch of Ystrad-Yw — the elder line being that of *Morgan of Llangeny.* The Church of Llanelly was dedicated to a daughter of Brychan who was named *Eilineth* or *Ellyned,* and it was anciently called *Llanellyned,* later abbreviated to *Llanelly.* It is a very old Church, with five bells, and outside is an old walled-in churchyard, with many ancient tombs. Within the Church there are quite a number of inscriptions on the walls and a communion table dedicated to members of the Lewis family. One of them, an Edward Lewis of Aberclydach gave two "charities" to the poor of the Parish and left gifts to pay for the preaching of sermons in Welsh. Aberclydach ("above the Clydach") is the ancient home-place of the family of Lewis of Llanelly. The author quotes from the Historian of this region: "I proceed to the later inhabitants of this tract, the most conspicuous of whom were the descendants of Rhys Goch, long settled at the old house at Aberclydach. Within the last century they were known by the name of

---

[68] *"A History of Brecknockshire"* by Theophilus Jones, pages 473-477.

LEWIS, but the elder branch of the family assumed that of Morgan, and resided at Llangeny as already noticed: the *Tref Pencenedl* of both is now Cwt-y-Gollen. The name of Lewis, however, remained here until late years, and now continues with one of the family settled at Pontypool." Mr., Jones, however, did not know that *one* very important branch of this ancient family had been transferred across the Seas to the Commonwealth of Virginia in 1653!

To carry on with the genealogical background of the Lewis of Llanelly family in Brecknockshire, one has only to examine the Pedigree of the father of Rhys Goch as given in *"The History of Monmouthshire"* under the heading of *MAENYRCH.* Sir Joseph Bradney was a native of Monmouthshire and most familiar with the background of the old families. Each generation of the line intermarried with a lady of arms-bearing pedigree. The mother of John Lewis was a *Catherine Morgan,* daughter of Watkin Morgan, Gent., of "Triley" in Llantilio Pertholey; his grandmother was *Nest* (an old Welsh name often given to the princesses of the royal lines), daughter and heiress to Thomas Philip Lewellyn of Llanelli (who also bore the Rhys Goch Coat-of-Arms); his great-grandmother was the daughter of Thomas Lewis John ap Gwilym of the de Turberville family seated at the Castle of Crickhowell in Brecon who were crossed with the Royal Line of Jestyn ap Gwrgant, Prince of Glamorgan; there were also heiresses of the families of Vaughan of Porthaml descended from Drimbenog, third son of Maenyrch; Price of Llanfoiste (descended from YNYR, King of Gwent); Havard of Portwyllym; two *Gunter* brides, of the family of Sir Peter Gaunt d'Or who came into Britain with William the Conqueror and who founded the prominent family of Gunter of Tregunter; the grandson of Rhys Goch, one *Idris ap Genillin,* married *ANNE* whose parents were *Moreiddig Warwyn,* Lord of Cantre-Self near Brecon (son to Drimbenog, youngest son of Maenyrch Lord of Brecknockshire) and *Elinor,* the daughter of The Lord Rhys of Deheubarth (Prince of South Wales). The Lord Rhys was a most unusual man — in fact, one of the most outstanding of his generation in that part of the world — a man who was an intimate friend of his enemy, Henry II the Plantagenet, and who ruled Wales in the latter's name. However, The Lord Rhys always maintained that the relationship between the English and the Welsh should *never* be that of "Master and Subject." He never submitted the sovereignty of his land. Then there was the bride of the son of Rhys Goch, *Genillin,* who married *Jenet,* daughter of Sir Howel of Caerlleon Castle; and there was *Joan* the wife of Rhys Goch, grand-daughter to *Elyston Glodrydd,* Earl of Hereford and Prince between the Wye and the Severn — one of the ancestors of the six

Royal Tribes of Wales; the wife of Maenyrch was *Elinor,* daughter to the Lord of Cantre-Self; finally, there was *Tegau Eufrom,* the legendary "golden breasted", wife to Caradawg Freichfras and daughter to King Pellinore — *"The Once and Future King."*[69] The line was strengthened in each generation by an infusion of equally fine blood-lines, so that it produced a truly illustrious line — one that is almost a subject of "hero-worship" in Wales, even today.

Then there comes to mind the contributions of this family along other lines. Howell Dda (910-950 A.D.) — known as "The Law-Giver". who reviewed and codified the Tribal Laws of the country and compiled them into the usable form that exists in part today. He traveled to Rome with his entire family, as the guest of the Emperor, and was there proclaimed as *"King of all the Welsh."* He was the grandfather of Rhys ap Tewdwr (grand-father of The Lord Rhys) and held his "seat" at Dinefawr Castle.[70] This Castle was later the stronghold of The Lord Rhys; the latter is noted for having founded at Cardigan in 1176 the remarkable *"Eisteddfod"* which continues even today and is a wonderful celebration of the native arts of all countries around the world and which meets each year in Wales. This combinaton of the Celtic Princelings and the Norman Knights produced a unique strain of people, quite different from other racial mixtures around the world. In many ways it contributed to the growth and greatness of the British Empire.

The line of *RHYS GOCH* is an illustrious one: it is descended from all six of the *"Royal Tribes of Wales"*.[71] *namely, (1) Gryffydd ap Cynan, King of Gwnyedd; (2) Rhys ap Tewdwr, King of Deheubarth; (3) Bleddyn ap Cynfyn, King of Powys; (4) Elystan Glodrudd, King of Rhwng Gwy ag Hafren* (between the Wye and Severn); *(5) Jestyn ap Gwrgant, King of Morgannwg;* and *(6) Ynyr, King of Gwent.* Most of the descent is on the "distaff" side, but "blood-wise" it is as authentic as the male descent, and it certainly produced an unusual strain. As a nation the Welsh were never really "conquered", but they were absorbed into the fabric of British life by a blend of the two cultures by intermarriage.

Before leaving the subject of the pedigree of Rhys Goch, it would seem fitting to discuss the matter of the *father of Rhys Goch.* There has been some doubt and disagreement as to whether or not Rhys Goch was the

---

[69] *"The Once and Future King"* by T. H. White and *"Arthurian Legends"* by Richard Barber, P. 207.

[70] *"Castles in Wales"* by the Welsh Tourist Board, Page 95.

[71] *"Royal and Princely Heraldry"* by Sir Anthony Wagner (1969), pages 10 and 11.

son of Maenyrch, Lord of Brecknock. The doubt arises from the fact that the ancient manuscripts and the *"Llyfr Baglan"* are also divided on this subject. Four pedigrees of the latter book *(pages 10, 141, 236, and 257)* claim Rhys Goch as the son of Maenyrch; whereas, two pedigrees *(pages 166 and 215)* assign *Rhys Goch as the son of Einion ap Gwage*. Mr. Peter C. Bartrum, the acknowledged authority on Welsh genealogy today, informed the author that the same variations occur in other manuscripts. In his *"Pedigrees of the Welsh Tribal Patriarchs"*[72] he lists four different descriptions of Rhys Goch's ancestry, the second of which is *"Rhys Goch ap Meinyrch anglwydd Ystrad Yw."* Documentation from the ancient manuscripts is given in each case.

Sir Joseph Alfred Bradney, in his *"History of Monmouthshire,"* on the Pedigree of Maenyrch,[73] places *Rhys Goch* as the second son of Maenyrch — the eldest being *Bleddyn* and the youngest being *Drimbenog* (or Trimbenog). It is a fact that *"The Llyfr Baglan"* has some material in it which cannot be fully documented and may obtain errors — the pedigrees having been handed down for centuries; however, the "bardic" system of recording genealogies was as accurate as it was possible to obtain at that time! Moreover, John Williams,[74] a native of Monmouthshire who compiled the volume from 1600-1607, was very familiar with that area which bordered on Brecon, and he was also a member of one of the oldest families and would have known all of them intimately — families which had cherished and preserved their genealogies and traditions carefully with pride. This John Williams recorded *four out of six* pedigrees giving the father of Rhys Goch as Maenyrch! The author realizes that Mr. Peter C. Bartrum is the acknowledged authority today on Welsh Genealogy, and she has a sincere respect for his opinion and a great appreciation for his help and direction in her research; he would have examined all available manuscripts on this subject, which were not available to the author. However, it all occurred a long while ago, and it is impossible to document precisely, and thus arrive at a definite conclusion — so *it must all rest on individual opinion.*

However, Mr. Bartrum was kind enough to verify the author's suggestion that, *at any rate*, the line of Rhys Goch goes back to Maenyrch on the *"distaff"* side and hence back to Caradawg Freichfras in King

---

[72] *"The National Library of Wales Journal"* - XIII, page 106.

[73] *"The History of Monmouthshire"*, Bradney, Vol. I, Pt. II, Pp. 338.

[74] *"Bulletin of the Board of Celtic Studies"*, Vol. 29, Pt. 5 (Nov. 1980), Page 156, by Mr. Peter C. Bartrum, on the subject of the author of the "Llyfr Baglan."

Arthur's time! *ANNE,* the daughter of *Moreiddig Warwyn,* Lord of Cantre-Self near Brecon, married *Idris ap Genillin.* She was the granddaughter of one Drimbenog, third son to Maenyrch of Brecknock, whose descent from his father has never been questioned. Her mother was a daughter of The Lord Rhys — of Deheubarth, Prince of South Wales — an outstanding Welshman! "Blood-wise" the line goes all the way back into the mists of Welsh Genealogy![75]

In addition to the claim of descent from *Drimbenog* (third son to Maenyrch), there is still another claim of descent from *Bleddyn* (the eldest son) and the last native Prince to rule Brecknock before the Normans came. This, again, is recorded by Bradney in his *"History",* in the Pedigree of the *POWELL Family*[76] *(de Bredwarden Line of Brecon). This Powell line is that of the mother of John Lewis — Catherine Morgan* who married *Lewis Prichard, second son of Richard Lewis of Llanelly* (Will 1628). Her mother was *Gwenllian,* the daughter of Rawling ap Watkin Fychan, who inherited the estate of Pen-y-Clawdd from *his* wife who was the daughter and sole heir of *Ralph ap Sitsyllt.* The Mother of Rawling ap Watkin Fychan was one *"Dyddgu"* (the lovely day) daughter to *Thomas ap Howell Llewellyn* who was descended from one *Einion Sais.* The latter was a famous person in the train of King Edward III who distinguished himself at the Battles of Poitiers and Crecy, for which he was awarded the "Coat-of Three Cocks" and lands. This Einion Sais ("the Englishman") is fifth in descent from Bleddyn,[77] heir to Brecknock. So it would appear that the antecedents of John Lewis of Virginia have a proven claim to the ancient pedigrees of the Lords of Brecknock!

It would be worthwhile at this point to list the various Pedigrees in the *"Llyfr Baglan"* bearing on the matter of the father of *Rhys Goch, Lord of Ystrad-Yw.* The author has carefully examined *all* the pedigrees mentioning Rhys Goch in this compilation. On pages 10, 235, 141 and 257 are noted the pedigrees of *"Ynyr, Vaghan, King of Gwent",* and in all cases it states that this Ynyr married one *"Gladis, daughter to Rhys ap Maynarch, Lord of Ystrad Yw."* On the pedigree of Ynyr on page 141, it is stated: *"Ynyr Vaghan (the younger), K. of G., married Gladic, daughter to Rees goz' ap maynarch, lord of Istrod-town;* she beareth (arms) — *"Sable a chevron argent, three speerheads argent languid."* This speaks of Gladic as the daughter of *Rhys Goch ap Maynarch,* restating the

---

[75] *"Llyfr Baglan",* page 111.
[76] *"The History of Monmouthshire"* (Bradney), Vol. I, Pt. I, page 97.
[77] *"Llyfr Baglan",* page 237.

relationship of her father to Maenyrch, and in addition it gives a description of her Coat-of-Arms, which is *not* that used by her father, Rhys Goch, but that used by her grandfather, Maenyrch, Lord of Brecknock, thus strengthening the claim of her father's descent from Maenyrch. It would surely seem likely that the Bards of King of Gwent would be knowledgeable and exact concerning the maternal line of their King.

On page 120 (folio 139) of the *"Llyfr Baglan"* is a Pedigree of Caradawg Freichfras, ancestor of Maenyrch, back fourteen generations from the latter, and this pedigree ends with *"Hydd, the father of Driffin, the father of Maenyrch."* It goes on to state: *"This Maenyrch, being lord of Brecknock, had issue — Bleddyn ap Maynarch, Driffyn and Drympenock."* It will be noted that the father of Maenyrch was one *Driffin* and that Maenyrch's second son is given in this pedigree as *Driffyn*. It seemed logical that Maenyrch would name a son for his father — this is the only pedigree where this designation occurs. Therefore, it would appear possible to the author that the name *"Rhys Goch (meaning "red-haired"), the name always given to the Lord of Ystrad-Yw, could have been* a "nickname" for *Driffin,"* such as was the case in William Rufus or Richard the Lion-hearted. However, again, it all occurred a long time ago, so, *it, too, must rest on individual opinion.*

Also, on page 229 of the *"Llyfr Baglan"* (folio 290) is listed *"Certain Cotts as Heare followeth":* This is the Coat-of-Arms of *"Bleddyn ap Maynarch"* — eldest son and heir of Maenyrch, Lord of Brecknock. His Coat is thus: *"beareth sable and argent quarterid, a chevron argent three speer hedes argent languid on the first; a dragon's head azur with a man's hand in her mouth, the third as the second and the fourth as the first."* This description of the Coat of Bleddyn ap Maenyrch combines the Coat of his father, Maenyrch, with the Coat used by Rhys Goch; which would indicate that the second and third Coat (that of the dragon and hand) derived from the mother of Bleddyn — who would also have been the mother of Rhys Goch, whose Coat-of-Arms the latter used as his own. This Coat of Bleddyn definitely proves a blood relationship to Rhys Goch — and the "time" element involved verifies that they were contemporaries. Bleddyn died at "Battle" in 1090, and all the histories give the birth of Rhys Goch as around 1070. This statement of the *"Llyfr Baglan"* appears to verify the descent of Rhys Goch from Maenyrch, Lord of Brecknock.

Finally, on page 98 (folio 107) of this book under the title of *"Brecknock"* one finds the pedigree of Maynarch, Lord of Brec', giving his lineage back to Caradawg Freichfras. It reads: *"he beareth quarterlie S.*

et A., a Chevron A., 3 speres heades A., a dragon's head with a man's hand in his mouth, the three as one, the fourth as the second." These are the arms specifically assigned to Caradawg Freichfras in the first and third quarters *and* the arms assigned to Rhys Goch in the second and fourth. As Caradawg Freichfras is the acknowledged ancestor of Maenyrch, Lord of Brecknock, and the quartered arms assigned to the former are identical to those assigned to Rhys Goch, there does not seem to be any doubt but that the line goes through Rhys Goch, through Maenyrch, on fourteen generations to Caradawg. There appears to be more instances of this descent than from any others — both by pedigrees and by arms!

In conclusion, this was the heritage that John Lewis brought with him to the New World! The Lewis family lived in Virginia, much as they had in Wales; they were "country gentlemen" living on the land. They did not wish to become "entrepreneurs" of commerce and politics, as did the families of *Carter* and *Lee*, but they were content to live quietly and pleasantly, although not shunning their obligations in the affairs of Gloucester County. They were active in the Church of Abingdon, being Vestrymen and giving the Communal Service to that Church. They supported the defense of the County, when necessary, as officers in the County Militia. At the time of the Revolution the head of the Warner Hall Family, Warner Lewis, was made the Chairman of the Committee of Safety of Gloucester County. One member of that family, Colonel Fielding Lewis of Fredericksburg, who married General George Washington's sister, Betty, supplied the Rebel Army with most of the cannon used in that War. The grandson of the Emigrant John Lewis married Elizabeth, daughter and chief heir to Colonel Augustine Warner II; her mother was Mildred Reade of Yorktown, daughter of Colonel George Reade who had come to Virginia quite early and who replaced Governor Harvey as "Acting Governor" when the latter was recalled. The "seat" of the Warner Family — "Warner Hall" — became the traditional home of the Lewis family of Gloucester. Elizabeth's sister, Mildred, married Lawrence Washington, and they became the grandparents of the famous General; another sister, Mary, married Major John Smith "of Purton" in Gloucester County, and became an ancestress of the present Dowager Queen of England, Lady Elizabeth Bowes-Lyon, who, therefore, is "eighth" cousin to the present generation of the Lewis Family of Warner Hall. Another interesting family connection is that of Elizabeth Warner Lewis' Aunt — Sarah Warner, who married Lawrence Townley and became the ancestress of the famed General Robert E. Lee of the Confederacy. The grandfather of Elizabeth Warner Lewis, George Reade of

44

Yorktown, was descended from the DYMOKE LINE in England, traditional *"Champions of the Throne of England."* There is a Lewis home in Virginia called *"Marmion"* after a similar one in England. This family traces descent from the Conquest of Britain.

Besides *"Warner Hall"*, other secondary homes in Gloucester County were *"Belle Farm"* (now transported to the Williamsburg Community), *"Abingdon," "Land's End"* and others. The family called the river by "Warner Hall" — the *Severn* — to remember their place of origin in Wales, and they undoubtedly brought with them the first of the many Daffodil Bulbs which have spread all over the county and are an outstanding feature of that area each Spring. The yellow Daffodil is the "National Flower" of Wales. It should be remembered that the *Lewis and Clarke Exploration Team* which opened up the whole western part of the North American continent for the United States was headed by a member of the Lewis family — one Meriwether Lewis, a "cousin" from the Belvoir Branch of this family, a Cadet of the Gloucester family. Members of the family have served in every war of the country, most proudly in the War Between the States, when the County was devastated by the Peninsula Campaign of that disastrous war. The Confederate Statue to the memory of the Confederate Veterans who gave their lives for the State stands in front of the Gloucester Courthouse and it bears the name of the great-grandfather of the author of this treatise, THOMAS JEFFERSON HENDERSON of "The Gloucester Invincibles," from Eastern Shore of Virginia, who married Elizabeth Frances Lewis, daughter of George Washington Lewis of Gloucester County.

The family in Virginia carried on the traditions and asperations of the Lewis family of Brecon, and we have every reason to be proud of both!

Finally, the author would like to quote from a letter from Dr. Susan J. Davies, dated 29 January, 1984: *"Your established line of descent, via the heraldry, the tombstones, the Llantilio registers and the wills you have, is already much stronger than most people of ancient lineage in Wales are able to set on paper."* However, since that date, with the help of Dr. Davies' fine research in Wales, we have been able to add to that foundation the research in Abergavenny records — resulting from the research in Bradney's *"Notes"*, the *"Fines"*, the *"Covenants,"* and the *"Rentals,"* etc. Everything that exists to date has been covered and evaluated, and the author feels confident that at long last the truth has come to light — the genealogical world will now know the background of one of Virginia's most prominent lines!

KING ARTHUR AND CARADAWG FREICHFRAS,
KNIGHT OF THE ROUND TABLE

Since the author intends to carry the Lewis of Gloucester County, Virginia, genealogy back to Caradawg Freichfras, a Knight of the Round Table of King Arthur, it is essential to this genealogical treatise to authenticate the actual existence of Arthur as a *real person*, and not as some purely mythological character.

The story of King Arthur and his Knights of the Round Table is the glory of the British race and the delight of childhood.. It has spread from the British Isles, first into Brittany, then to France, Italy and Germany — even to the Far East. It has been the source of the inspiration, and the genesis of much of the great literature and music, of the continent of Europe, and has left its mark on all phases of human endeavor!

For centuries there has been a division of opinion among scholars as to whether or not King Arthur was a legendary figure of Romance, or whether he was truly an historical personage of early Britain. The only just manner at which to arrive at a conclusion — after a lapse of nearly fifteen hundred years — is to weigh all the evidence available and make a clear evaluation of the *facts.*

Did Arthur ever live? While the idea of a King Arthur whose dominions extended beyond the confines of the British Isles is now generally rejected, we may probably accept as a fact the existence of a chieftain of mixed British and Roman lineage (witness the Latin names in his pedigree) who had learned the art of war from the Romans (particularly the use of horses and cavalry in battle) and successfully led the forces of the minor British kings against the Saxon invaders.[1] It now remains to present *the known facts concerning the historicity of King Arthur.*

The most outstanding piece of evidence on this matter[2] is to be found

---

[1] *"The Encyclopaedia Britannica"* (1935), Vol. 2, P. 461.
[2] *"The Mystery of King Arthur"* (1975), by Elizabeth Jenkins, Pp. 28 and 29.

in a bundle of documents kept in the British Museum labeled *"Historical Miscellany."* Included among these documents is a set known as *"The Easter Annals."* These records were kept in the Monasteries, as a necessity of life, during that period of history when Europe was enveloped in the "Dark Ages." The "Annals" were needed because Easter is a *moveable feast,* and it was necessary to draw up calculations as to when it would fall for the next given number of years. *"The Annals"* were arranged in columns and the right-hand column was left blank; in this, were noted down, events of outstanding importance.. The entries in these columns are called — *"The Easter Annals."* It is accepted that the date of a manuscript containing the Annals is considerably later than that of the events noted in the Annals; but the experts are agreed that, when the new tables of calculation were drawn up, the chief events from the previous tables were carried over to the current ones. The two vital entries occurring in these "Annals" are (1) *"The Battle of Badon, in which Arthur carried the Cross of the Lord Jesus Christ on his shoulders for three days and nights and the Britons were victorious."* The date of the entry is either 499 or 518 A.D., depending upon the interpretation of the scribe's method; and (2) *"The Battle of Camlann, in which Arthur and Modred perished. And there was plague in Britain and Ireland."* The validity of these facts is further substantiated and verified by the English author, Leslie Alcock,[3] in his book on King Arthur. It appears self-evident that Arthur really did exist!

These facts were reiterated further by a number of learned scholars who sought to perpetuate the fame of this early Briton. The Latin literary culture of Europe fled to the British Isles at the onset of the "Dark Ages", and flourished there in the monasteries. One such exponent was an "ecclesiastic" named *"Gildas,"* writing in 550 A.D., *almost contemporary with King Arthur!* His work is entitled: *"Gildas Sapiento de excidio et conquestu Britannica,"* and in the history section of his writings he lists the achievements of Arthur. In an authoritative article on the subject of Medieval Literature,[4] it is stated; "In the sixth Century Gildas is our authority for the last days of Roman Britain." If Gildas was the authority for that period, then surely he was the authority for the period of his own lifetime — that of King Arthur! So we could accept his statement *that the Battle of Badon actually took place,* with its subsequent victory of Arthur over the Saxons. Gildas further states that the

---

[3] *"Arthur's Britain: History and Archaeology"* (1972), Pp. 367-464.
[4] *"The Encyclopaedia Britannica"* (1935), Vol. 13, P. 754.

Battle took place at the time of his own birth, which would make it around 516 A.D. Thus it would seem from the writings of Gildas that Arthur was a very real person, historically. Gildas describes the Battle of Badon in detail, as "almost the last slaughter of the enemy (Saxons) —an event of singular importance in that age."[5]

The next verification of Arthur came in the mid-eighth Century from a Welsh Monk named *Nennius*. in his *"Historia Britonum"* he claims, "I heaped together all that I found from the annals of the Romans, the writings of the holy men (Monks), and the traditions of our old men." He also mentions that Arthur, leading the rulers of the small British kingdoms, was victorious over the Saxons, and preserved what was left of Roman civilization and Christianity, at least for the time being. Nennius calls Arthur — *"Miles"* — a soldier, and that is probably about the truth of his original role. It is evident that the reputation of this renowned person was enlarged and embroidered upon by subsequent generations and centuries, but this was obviously accomplished on the fabric of "truth" of his actual existence and deeds! Finally, we must remember than Nennius lived less than two hundred years from Arthur's greatest glory — so that it would not have been unusual that he was able and anxious to record proudly the exploits of this great man!

The best authority states: "Our sources for the historical Arthur are (1) *"The Historia Britonum"* of Nennius; (2) *"The Annales Cambriae"* of an unknown author, written shortly after 965 A.D.; and (3) *"The Gesta Regum"* of William of Malmesbury, completed in 1125 A.D.[6] Both of the latter also connected Arthur with the Battle of Badon.

Other writers have added to the story of Arthur, such as Maistre Wace in his *"Geste des Bretons;"* also, Geoffrey of Monmouth (who, incidentally was a native of the same section of Wales where King Arthur had one of the three seats of government in his time — namely, Caerlleon-on-Usk). In his *"Historia Britonum"*, written in 1147 A.D., he became the source of most of the later biographies and accounted for much of the exaggeration of the legend, as he added the mythological aspect to the story; then there was Layamon, writing in the Anglo-Saxon language, who told a unique story — "To him, it was not only a story, it was a faith." He inspired most of the later legends which swept across Europe, bringing forth beautiful literature in every country. To the story of Arthur, Layamon added an aura of chivalry, a code of honor, and a

---

[5] *"The Mystery of King Arthur"* (1975), by Elizabeth Jenkins, P. 28.
[6] *"The Encyclopaedia Britannica"* (1935), Vol. 2, p. 459.

national pride! All these literary efforts culminated in the glorious *"Idylls of the King"* by Alfred Lord Tennyson, which most of us remember as the high-light of our childhood and youth . . . .

There are several other modern books which deal with this fascinating subject (for, indeed, it has recently become highly popular) of King Arthur and his Knights. The first is *"The Quest for Arthur's Britain"*, edited by Geoffrey Ashe and published by the Granada Publishing Company, first in 1971. Mr. Ashe, appears convinced of the historicity of Arthur, for he writes: "From a strange medley of clues, patiently pieced together in the last forty or fifty years, one certainty at least emerges. The Arthurian legend, however wide-ranging in its vagaries, is rooted in *Arthurian Fact*. As the legend is unique, so the fact is unique. In essence, it is this. Britain, alone among the lands of the Roman Empire, achieved independence before the northern barbarians poured in, and put up a fight against them — a very long, and at one stage, a successful fight. Between Roman Britain and Anglo-Saxon England, there is an inter-regnum, which is not a chaos as historians once imagined, but a creative epoch with a character of its own. This rally of a Celtic people, in some degree Romanized and Christianized, is the reality of Arthur's Britain. It occurs in a dark age, the mysterious gap in British history. The modern investigator's problem is to bring light into the darkness — where it may, possibly, reveal the features of Arthur himself." Mr. Ashe bases most of his beliefs and verifications upon rather recent archaeological exploration and "finds" in the areas involved in Arthur's history. He states several positions which strengthen the genealogical study of this period and area; one is in a sentence — *"Both Belli and Bran occur in the pedigrees of several Welsh families."* Belli is listed in the Pedigree of Brychan, Lord of Brecheiniog.[7] And also, Mr. Ashe, further states: *"Several Welsh genealogies look plausible even as far back as the fifth century."*[8] *(The author of this treatise has carried the genealogies of four or more of the most outstanding families of Wales back into the fifth century.)* Among these are Lewis, Bredwarden, Price, Vaughan, Meredith, Wogan and Lloyd — all come from the line of Maenyrch father of RHYS GOCH of Ystrad Yw, Brecknockshire; it is highly unlikely that those families would have independently perpetuated the descent of their "Family Tree" (Pedigree) from Caradawg Freichfras, a Knight of King Arthur's Round Table, unless it were true and had been

---

7 *"The Quest for Arthur's Britain"* (1971), edited by Geoffrey Ashe, P. 35.
8 *"Ibid."*, P. 169.

treasured in their family records for centuries. Thus it is this author's considered opinion that both King Arthur and Caradawg Freichfras (Knight of the Round Table) really *did* exist, and that the families mentioned before were so proud of their descent from the latter, that they would never allow the truth to die.

Mr. Ashe writes thoroughly of the "digs" at Tintagel (Birthplace of King Arthur), Dinas Powys, Caerlleon and Glastonbury Tor — and others — and the archaeological remains found in these historic spots lend much authenticity to the reality of the subject. He believes that "the spade has filled the gaps which the pen left open." When one remembers that most of the earliest history of the human race has been verified and recorded from archaeological discoveries, one is more than prone to agree with Mr. Ashe.

Finally, the second modern publication in the field of Arthur should be mentioned here; it is entitled: *"History of the Kings of Britain"* by Geoffrey of Monmouth; translated by Sebastian Evans from the Welsh into English in 1903; it has been revised by Charles W. Dunn, a Celtic scholar from Canada. It covers the twelve books of *"The Mabinogion"*, and states that practically our only reliable picture of Arthur is shown in the story of *Culhwch and Olwen,* a tale adopted from *"The Red Book of Hergest."* And now, having reviewed the most important sources concerning this most interesting period of British history, it is time to move on to the genealogical aspect of this treatise.

The most recognized authority of later Welsh genealogy is the splendid *"History of Monmouthshire"* published in 1906 by Sir Joseph Alfred Bradney. This book was recommended to the author by the National Library of Wales at Aberystwyth and quoted to her by several eminent authorities in that country. Sir Joseph himself was amply qualified for the task he undertook, being a Fellow of the Society of Antiquarians, Bachelor of Arts of Trinity College, Cambridge, a Justice of the Peace, Deputy-Lieutenant, and County Councillor of the County of Monmouth. On page 338 of Volume I, Pt. II, dealing with the Hundred of Abergavenny, he cites the generation immediately before RHYS GOCH, ancestor of the Lewis family of Virginia. This generation is headed by *MAENYRCH, LORD OF BRECHEINIOG,* whom he states is fourteenth in descent from Caradawg Freichfras, Lord of Gloucester and Fferlis, and Knight of the Round Table. He gives the three sons of Maenyrch as (1) *Bleddyn* who inherited from the father and who was slain at "Battle" in 1090 by Bernard de Newmarsh, the Norman who conquered Brecknock; (2) *Rhys Goch* (about 1070), the second son of Maenyrch is known as Lord of Ystrad Yw. He and his descendants lived in the Parish of Llanelly, on the border between Monmouthshire and Brecknock. From him descend in the female line several prominent Welsh families, but the only one to descend in the male line is *LEWIS OF LLANELLY*,[9] from whom derives the line of John Lewis of Gloucester County, Virginia. The Arms of Rhys Goch, and those of the Lewis Family of Gloucester, are identical; the third son, *Tymbenog* became the ancestor of the outstanding Vaughan and de Bredwarden families.

Caradawg Freichfras* is given on this Pedigree as a *Knight of the Round Table* of King Arthur. His wife was named *Tegau Eufrom*, daughter of King Pelynor. His arms are stated to be: *"Sable, a chevron between three spear-heads, embrued gules."* He is claimed as an ancestor by a number of Welsh families tracing back to the fifth or fourth century. The wife of Maenyrch is given as *Elinor*, daughter to Einion ap Selif. Following this information, Sir Joseph proceeds with the Pedigree through Rhys Goch, down to the Lewis of Llanelly family of Dan-y-Parc.

It seems necessary, at this point, to explain how these wonderful records of many centuries were preserved and perpetuated through all that time! One must understand the structure of the *Bardic System* of the Celtic peoples of Britain, upon whom these ancient records must rest. The organization and position of the Bards in Wales (and Ireland and Scotland) in the social and political life of the country seems peculiar to the Celts. The Bards were an honored and important group of persons, and their work became the *unwritten history* of their people. The Bards were divided into three groups — (1) the upper grade (or "Chief of Song") whose duty it was to sing the praises and deeds of his Lord and the Lord's family; he was present at every important occasion of birth, marriage and death, and recounted the genealogy of the family and connections. (2) Next came the "Bards of the King's Guards", who did for the King's household what the former did for the King himself; last of all (3) were "Musicians" who were permitted more freedom than the other two, both in form and subject matter, sometimes going into the ribald and satire. From the work of the latter group evolved the famous *"Mabinogion"*—a word derived from the plural of *Mabigon* which means "a Bard's apprentice." The Bards were highly respected and in a class by themselves. To obtain admission into the ranks of this Bardic hierarchy, a candidate must undergo a strict and definite literary training; he must prove himself master of certain traditional lore. This assured a continuation of the knowledge and traditions of the people.

---

9 *"History of Monmouthshire"*, Vol. I, Pt. II, P. 327.

Even as late as Henry IV a session of Bards was held to bestow certificates of proficiency and to keep the standards high. Bardism often went by families, and this fact alone led to the continuance of the best of the system. They were, however, allowed to recite the tales they knew for pay — it was a profession!

Out of the tales of the Bards — handed down for generations — grew *"The Mabinogion"* — often called by the authorities — "Juvenile Tales". They related the earliest, most important experiences of the Race and because of them, Wales became the genesis for Medieval Literature in Europe. These tales were translated from the ancient Welsh into English in the middle of the last century by Lady Charlotte Guest; her effort was highly praised by Sir Samuel Rush Meyrick, Editor of the *"Herald's Visitation to Wales"* — who described her work as "exquisite."[10] The third section of *"The Mabinogion"* included stories about King Arthur and his Knights — and some tales go back as far as the Roman administration of Wales. Lady Charlotte, in doing her translation, set for herself a high standard — "to preserve in Anglo-Saxon English the primitive simplicity of the Welsh original." On page 8 of the "Original Introduction" to *"The Mabinogion"*, Lady Charlotte writes: "The Welsh possessed an ancient literature, containing various lyric compositions, and certain triads, in which are arranged *historical facts and aphorisms* . . . . . . the high antiquity of many of these compositions." These tales formed the basis of much of the Medieval Literature of the continent — making Wales the cradle of European Romance!

In *"The Dream of Rhonaby"*, the eighth tale of *"The Mabinogion"*, on page 141, one finds the only known description of Caradawg Freichfras. The scene is the assembling of the troops before King Arthur, prior to the Battle of Badon. I quote from the original: "Then spoke a tall and stately man, of noble and flowing speech, saying that it was a marvel that so vast a host should be assembled in so narrow a space and that it was a still greater marvel that those should be there at that time who had promised to be by mid-day in the Battle of Badon, fighting with Osla Gyllellvwr. 'Whether thou mayest proceed or not, I will proceed.' "Thou sayest well," said Arthur, "and we will go altogether." "Iddawc," said Rhonaby, "Who was the man who spoke so marvelously unto Arthur?"[11] *"A man who may speak as boldly as he listeth, Caradawc*

---

[10] *"The Herald's Visitation to Wales"* by Lewys Dwnn (1586-1613), P. 10.
[11] *"The Mabinogion"* Notes, page 343, "Iddawc is found in the Catalogue of Welsh Saints."

Freichfras, the son of Llyr Marini, his chief counselor, and his cousin." This is the first indication of the relationship between Caradawc and Arthur; as their fathers were from two different families, then the "cousin" connection must have come from their mothers' side. In "The Notes" accompanying the translation, on pages 346 and 347, is a descriptive background of Caradawg. It reads: "Caradawc, like Trystan, and many other heroes whose names occur in *"The Mabinogion",* was celebrated both in Wales and Norman story. He was the son of Llyr Merini, a Prince of Cornwall, and himself a Chief Elder of Arthur at Celliwig, the Royal Residence in that part of the Island. His mother was *GWEN*, grand-daughter of Brychan, through whose right he is supposed to have become the ruler of the district of Brycheiniog."

According to *"The Triads"[12]* he was one of the Battle Knights of Britain, and in an Englyn(Elegy) attributed to Arthur himself, Caradawc is styled as "Caradawc, pillar of the Cymry (Welsh)". Several other interesting facts are known about Caradawc. His wife was Tegau Eufrom — the "Golden Breasted", who was renowned for her virtue, as well as her beauty. His horse was named *"Lluagor"* — "Host-splitter". His identifying name of "Freichfras" (sometime called Vreichfras) means *"Brawny-Arm."* In a letter from Dr. Constance Bulloch-Davies, an authority on Arthurian Legend, it is stated by her that this epithet, or name, "Freichfras", is the *one thing* which separates Caradawc from others of the same name. Finally, Lady Charlotte Guest definitely states on page 347 of *"The Mabinogion"* that *"Several Welsh families trace their Pedigrees to Caradawg."*

The two battles of Arthur which have identified him as historical —Badon and Camlann — are also recounted in *"The Mabinogion".[13]*

On page 39 of The Notes (page 103 of the original) is an article on the geography of the name *Gelliwig* (home of Caradawc in Cornwell); it is sometimes written *Gelli Wic.* Here Caradawc was "Chief Elder" of Arthur — and the place was one of three seats of government of the King. The site of Gelliwig today is somewhat in doubt, but one authority places it at *Callington* (Kellington or Killiwick). It may be taken as some confirmation of this point in regard to the location of Gelliwig, that there is a place in the vicinity of Callington still bearing the appellation of "Arthur's Hall." Near to the Hall are many rocky basins, called by the common people "Arthur's troughs", and which, according to tradition, that monarch used to feed his dogs.

---

[12] The "most unusual" of personages and things in groups of three. (Triads)
[13] Pages 141 and 138.

Caradawc is said to have died at the Battle of *Cattraeth,* in 546 A.D., in which 360 Knights participated and only three survived. The prowess of this warrior is sung in verse by his contemporary, Aneurin, who calls on several of his fellow-warriors in evidence of his assertion.[14] I quote from the verse;

> "When Caradawg rushed into battle,
> It was like the tearing onset of the woodland boar,
> The bull of combat in the field of slaughter,
> He attracted the wild dogs by the action of his hand,
> My witnesses are Owain the son of Eulat,
> And Gwrien, and Gwynn, and Gwriat.
> From Cattraeth and its carnage,
> From the battle encounter,
> After the clear bright mead was served'
> He saw no more the dwelling of his father."

Lady Charlotte's translation of the renowned *"Mabinogion"* is valuable, not only for the many historical facts verified throughout it, but for the description of the life, habits, morals and mores of that time. It contains a wealth of knowledge — both historical, legendary, and mythological. It is a joy to read!

The author has been exceedingly fortunate in her correspondence with outstanding authorities on the subject of Caradawg Freichfras. She asked each authority for his or her opinion of the interpretation of the records — for, as Dr. Rachel Bromwich wrote in a letter, "At this point of time you are quite right in saying that an 'an opinion' is the most that anyone can give on the question of his possible historicity." Dr. Bromwich is the distinguished author of *"Trioedd Ynys Prydein,"*[15] a most scholarly dissertation on the *"Triads of Wales."* She gives the Welsh original and the English translation in her remarkable book. Caradawg Freichfras is mentioned several times in the Triads — *first* — on page 1, in Triad number one — *"Three Tribal Thrones of the Island of Britain* — Arthur as Chief Prince in Celliwig in Cornwall, and Bishop Bytwini as Chief Bishop, and *Caradawg Strong-Arm as Chief Elder;" second —* on page 31, in Triad number eighteen, *"Three Battle-Horsemen of the Island of Britain." — Caradawg Strong-Arm,* and Menwaedd of Arl-

---

[14] *'Myvyrian Archiology",* Vol. I, P. 5 and "Notes, page 347.
[15] *"Trioedd Ynys Prydein"* - "The Welsh Trials", edited with Introduction, Translation and Commentary by Rachel Bromwich, University of Wales Press, Cardiff, 1978, pages 299 and 300.

lechwedd, and Llyr of the Hosts; eighteen W — "Three Favorites of Arthur's Court, and Three Battle Horsemen; they would never endure a *Penteulu* over them. And Arthur sang an englyn (Poem): "These are my Three Battle Horsemen — Menedd and Ludd of the Breastplate, *and the Pillar of Cymry, Caradawg;" third* — on pages thirty-eight and thirty-nine, in Triad number thirty-eight,

> "Three Bestowed Horses of the Island of Britain;
> Slender Grey, horses of Caswallawn son of Belli,
> Pale Yellow of the Stud, horse of Lleu Skillful Hand,
> and *Host-Splitter, horse of Caradawg Strong-Arm.* "

The importance of horses to the Welsh at this time in history is evidenced by the use of the cavalry, which Arthur learned from the Roman occupation. In fact, it is believed that the Battle Steeds of his Knights were the result of the inter-breeding of the War-horses of the Romans and the Welsh ponies, each contributing to the characteristics of the steeds later used in combat and jousts. Another name for "Host-Splitter" was *"Luagor"*, and the Triads indicate that he was conceived at the same time as Caradawg and was his companion in all adventures; the *fourth* mention of Caradawg in the *Triads* is number seventy-two, on pages 189 and 190. *"Three Surpassing Bonds of Enduring Love which three Men formerly in the time of Arthur cast upon the Three Fairest, most Lovable, and most Talked-of Maidens who were in the Island of Britain at that time; that is (the bond) which Tristan son of Tallweh cast upon Essylit daughter of (Culfanawyd) Pillar of Britain; and the (bond) which Cynon son of Clydno Eiddyn cast upon Morfudd daughter of Urien Rheged; and the (bond) which Caradawg Strong-Arm son of Llyr Marini cast upon Tegau "Gold-Breast" daughter of Nudd Generous-Hand, King of the North. And those were the Fairest, Most Lovable, and most Talked-of Maidens who were in the Island of Britain at that time. "*

Dr. Bromwich gave her opinion that "Caradawg Freichfras was a Hero of Romance — legendary, rather than historical." However, she states that he was an early one, probably much more prominent in the early oral Arthurian tradition than in later times, and she cited the number of Triads which refer to him. The author believes that she is viewing the question mostly as an authority on medieval Welsh literature at that period, for the truth seems to be that legend, literature and history appear to be inextricably inter-twined!

Another Arthurian authority with whom the author consulted was Dr. Constance Bulloch-Davies of the Department of Classics, University of North Wales at Bangor. She praised the work of Dr. Bromwich in all respects; her one difference of opinion was that she referred to Caradawg as the ancestor of the Lords, or rulers, of Morgannwg (Glamorganshire). She stressed the point that the identifying feature was in the name *"Freichfras"* — eliminating all others of the same name of Caradawg.

It is necessary to mention one other publication of *"The Triads"* —that of the compilation of Iolo Morgannwg, translated by W. Probert. This is a more popular, paper-back edition — and it deals with the literary aspect — not strictly adhering to historical and scholarly standards.

Lastly, we come to a most important source concerning Caradawg Freichfras! This is *"The Heraldic Visitation of Wales and Part of the Marches."* Between the years 1596 and 1613, under the authority of Clarencius and Norroy, Two Kings of Arms, *LEWIS DWNN*, Deputy Herald at Arms, compiled and transcribed from the original manuscripts and charters in the Monasteries, from the Pedigrees of all the prominent families of Wales, and from all available ancient chronicles of the "old men", all information concerning the lineage of the families of Wales. It was a tremendous undertaking,, and one which was accomplished with a great deal of care and exactness. In fact, authorities have stated that his work compares most favorably with that of the College of Arms records in London. Lewys Dwnn was a member of one of the prominent families of Wales; he was fluent in both Welsh and English, and he was duly accredited and commissioned by the College of Arms. His Pedigrees, which he obtained from the "Heads" of the various families, were duly "signed" as correct by the Head of each Family. In 1846, Sir Samuel Rush Meyrick, Knt., K.H. LLD. F.A.S., gathered together all the manuscripts of Lewys Dwnn and edited them with accompanying "Notes" of explanation. This compilation was published by the *Welsh Manuscript Society* and printed by W. Rees. The author has the privilege of having the first volume of this compilation in her own library to peruse at leisure, and Xerox prints of both volumes from the Library of Congress helped immeasureably. The text of Lewys Dwnn is in Welsh — a most difficult language — but the Notes are in English.

The author has abstracted various Pedigrees from these volumes — specifically those dealing with the "descent from Caradawg Freichras." On page 190 of Volume I is the Pedigree of the *Vaughan* Family, entitled: *"Bredwardin of Herefordshire"*. It includes a descent from Caradawc Vreichfras, Earl of Hereford, by Tegau Aufrom. (This Pedigree is also found in the Visitations of the Counties of Wilts and Hereford, in the time of the reigns of James I and Charles I) The Vaughan

Family descend in the female line from Maenyrch, through his third son, TYMBENOG, (or Drimbenog) ARGLWYDD Y KWMWD AP MAENARCH. The Pedigree back of Maenyrch is given as "Maenyrch ap *Tryfen varfog* ap *Hydd* ap *Gwyngudd* ap *Anarawd* ap *Terghy* ap *Tethwal* ap *Keindeg* ap *Kynfarch* ap *Hoiw* ap *Gloiw* ap *Kawrds* ap *Kradog vraichfraisg.* "This represents thirteen generations, instead of the fourteen given in the Maenyrch Pedigree in *"The History of Monmouthshire"* by Sir Joseph Alfred Bradney. In the "Introduction" to the "Visitations" by Sir Samuel Meyrick, he quotes from *Guttin Owen* (a celebrated poet and genealogist) the generations back of Caradawc — and they are: "Cariadoc *freichfras,* ap *Llier Merini,* ap *Engion Yrth,* ap *Cynedda weldic.* "This carries the lineage of Caradawg back three more generations, to about 400 A.D. or the fifth century.

Then in Book II, pages 56 and 57, one finds the Pedigree of *Gwhelyth ap* Henry (Folio Number 108) — listed as *Lewis ab Wm Howell of Abergwyly,* who married one Jenet, daughter and heir to Morgan Jenkin; this pedigree is traced back to Kradog Vreichfras, "Earl of Ferlex and Prince between the Wye and Severn, Lord of ye Dolorous Tower and Knight of the Round Table in King Arthur's time, lynially descended from Belli ye Great emprour (sic.) of Great Britain." These lineages are given to show the various family pedigrees in Wales who maintain a descent from Caradawc Freichfras. The spelling of the proper names may vary in some instances, but it is possible to trace the descent without doubt.

Then, in Book II, page 36, is the *Pedigree of Brecheiniog Porthaml* which is also another branch of the family of Vaughan, and it goes back to Trymbenog, third son of Maenyrch, too; it carries the line back five generations from Caradawc — namely, *Llyr Myreini* ab *Merchio gil* ap *Gorwst Bedwlm* ab *Kemar* ab *Hoel Godebog.* Also mentioned in these pedigrees are other historical figures, such as Urien, King of Rheged. The pedigree of Vaughan of Porthand is verified in *"The History of Brecknockshire"* by the noted authority, Theophilus Jones, page 340.

On page XX of Book I is the Pedigree of Gwrydd ap Rhys Goch, one of the Fifteen Noble Tribes of North Wales. It reads: "Gwrydr Goch ap Helic ap Gwgon Gleddyfrudd ap Cariadoc freichfras ap Llir Merini ap Engion yrth ap Gyneddn Wledic." This is another confirmation of the pedigree of Rhys Goch and his descent from Caradawg — and even for the pedigree for three generations beyond Caradawg! This one was from *"Old Chronicles of Wales"* by the famous *Guttin Owen.* On page 48 of Book I is still another pedigree of Rhys Goch, Knt. The fact that not every generation is given, but the word "ap" used for connection between them, is explained on page 37 of this volume of the *"Visitations"*, when the Editor, Sir Samuel Meyrick, states: "This shows that "ap" often means "a descendant.""

In Book II of the *"Visitations,"* page 38, is found the *"Llyfr Achau"* —*"Book of Pedigrees'* — in which are noted the many famous personages of the Welsh Pedigrees and their lines of descent. One of these (Number 59), of these ancient manuscripts, deals with *LLywel* in Brecknockshire, and traces the pedigree of Brychan, Lord of Brecknock, down to HOWELL Dda, known to Wales as *"Law Giver"*. He was the King who compiled and codified the tribal laws of Wales and presented them to his people in a manner much of which is still in use today. He was known as "King of all the Welsh" (910-950). Howell Dda was a descendent of Rhodri Mawr (the Great) who held the advance of the Northmen pirates at bay (844-78), and also a descendent of Brychan whose grand-daughter, Gwen, was the mother of Caradawg Freichfras, These lineages are recounted in *"The Visitations."*

As quoted from the Introduction to these two wonderful volumes — the reason for which they were sponsored by and promoted by the Welsh Manuscript Society is as follows: "Formed for the purpose of transcribing and printing the more important of the numerous unpublished and Historical Remains of Wales." With such an objective in mind, the final result must certainly represent the most authentic and worthwhile records of those most remarkable people! The two volumes could hardly be endorsed by a more reliable authority!

Before closing this treatise on Caradawg Freichfras and his "cousin" King Arthur, the author wishes to acknowledge the help of the Curator of the Museum of Welsh Antiquities of the University College of North Wales. The Honorable John Ellis Jones of Bangor was most courteous in the time he gave to resolve my questions. In a letter of 31 January, 1983, he traced the form of the name of Karadawg — saying that it is generally accepted that the basic name is the Celtic form *Caratacus*, the name recorded by the Roman Historian Cornelius Tacitus, in his accounts of the Roman Conquest of Britain in his *"Annals"*, Book XII, chps. 33-37. He states that the form comes down to modern times as Caradog, or Cradog, which is a not uncommon name in Wales today —in fact, his own son bore the name! He also sent me the comments of the late Sir Idris Foster, sometime professor of Celtic at Oxford University, to whom he showed my questions. Sir Idris stated: "Caradawg Freichfras was an ancestor of one of the Fifteen Noble Tribes of Wales (a later Medieval classification of gentry families, with heraldic devices and the like, anachronistically ascribed to some of the 'founders') and so claimed as an ancestor by families who claimed descent from one of these Noble Tribes."

Then Mr. Jones went on to relate an amusing story which I shall repeat. He wrote: "In the last century were two eminent Welsh doctors, one a physician and the other a bone-specialist, of the same name, *THOMAS JONES,* and both knighted. One Sir Thomas Jones drew upon his legendary ancestor for a distinctive extra sur-name, and hit upon a tranlation of *Freichfras* — *ARMSTRONG:* Hence, *THE* Armstrong-Jones family, of whom one Anthony Armstrong Jones married Princess Margaret and so became Lord Snowdon." The Welsh have very long memories!

Thus, we bring the story of Caradawg Freichfras up to modern times. With the renewed interest in King Arthur and his Knights of the Round Table it is most fitting and remarkable to trace a Colonial Virginia Family back to this most unusual personage! The author has always felt that some of the best blood of the old country came to Virginia, and now it is apparently true!

ACKNOWLEDGEMENTS

The author is deeply appreciative of the encouragement, assistance and inspiration which was received from many kind persons during the preparation of this work. Among them are:

Dr. R. Geraint Gruffyd, B.A., D. Phil., Librarian of the National Library of Wales

Honorable Daniel Huws, Keeper of Manuscripts and Records at the National Library

Mr. R.W. McDonald, Assistant Keeper of Manuscripts and Records at the National Library

The Honorable John Ellis Jones, Curator of the Museum of Welsh Antiquities of the University College of North Wales

The late Sir Idris Foster, M.A., F.S.A. (former Professor of Celtic Studies at Oxford and later Vice-President of the National Library).

Dr. Peter C. Bartrum, noted authority of *"Welsh Genealogies"*

Dr. Michael Siddons, authority on Welsh Heraldry

Dr. Rachel Bromwich, acknowledged authority on the Arthurian period

Dr. Constance Bulloch-Davies, of the Classics Department, University of North Wales

Mr. Basil G. Twigg, Genealogist

Mr. Richard Barber, author of *"The Arthurian Legend"*

Miss Elizabeth Jenkins, author of *"The Mystery of King Arthur"*

Mrs. Laetitia Yeandle, Librarian of the Folger Shakespearean Library in Washington, D.C.

Mr. Thomas E. Wilgus, Reference Specialist of the Local History and Genealogy Section of the Library of Congress

Considerable thanks must be given to my friend, The Reverend Donald Francis, Vicar of St. Teilo's Church in Llantilio Pertholey, Gwent, who transcribed by hand *all* the Lewis entries in his ancient *"Register"* (from 1591-1640). Without his help and encouragement this work would have been impossible.

Lastly, but certainly not least, is the wonderful research which Dr. Susan J. Davies performed for the author at the National Library — her pains-taking, careful research brought to light documents which definitely proved the genealogical research on John Lewis of Virginia.

SUPPLEMENT

Corrections and Addenda to <u>The Welsh Lineage of John Lewis (1592-1657),</u> <u>Emigrant to Gloucester, Virginia</u> by Grace McLean Moses.

Further research on the genealogical background in Wales of the Warner Lewis Family of Gloucester, Virginia, has revealed several changes and additions to the original book which the author wishes to correct and make a part of the record for future generations. They are as follows:

Item 1 - This is the most important change, as it involves the wife of John Lewis, one Johane Lewis, whom he married at St. Teilo Church, Llantilio Pertholey Parish, Monmouthshire, on February 3rd, 1610. In the book her father was traced from one <u>William Lewis the Elder</u> of the Llanddewi Rhydderch family—and her mother as <u>Elizabeth Proger</u> of Wernddu in Llantilio Pertholey. This was deducted from available published records and from information sent by the professional genealogist, one Mr. Basil Twigg, whom I had commissioned to review and abstract the records of the National Library of Wales at Aberystwyth. Later he was commissioned to travel to St. Teilo and examine and abstract the Lewis entries in the ancient "Register." Working with these various sources, the only possible father of Johane Lewis was the above-mentioned William Lewis. However, a close perusal of his WILL and that of his son, William Lewis the Younger, developed that the interpretation of this genealogy was incorrect.

The author was most fortunate to receive a photostatic copy of the precious "Register" of St. Teilo which began in the year 1591/92 (Old Style). On the first page was the entry of the Baptism of "<u>John, son of Lewis Rycketts February 10th, 1591/2,</u>" Mr. Twigg, the professional genealogist, explained that the <u>Rycketts</u> could very well be a colloquialism for <u>Richards</u>, which in turn could be <u>Prichard</u>—this was the name the sons of Richard Lewis of Llangattuck-nigh-Uske used in his WILL of 1627/28. Upon further examination a name was discovered which <u>had not</u> been forwarded by the genealogist. This name was RICHARD LEWIS who appeared in the "Register" as the Curate and Vicar for the years 1612-1614, signing the yearly report on Births, Marriages and Burials in Latin, which would indicate that he had been trained as a priest. The only other entry in his name was that of his death as <u>Richard Lewis, Clerk, buried Nov. 13, 1617.</u>

Now the question arose—"Who was this Richard Lewis?" Dr. Susan J. Davies, the second researchist, recommended to replace Mr. Twigg, began to resolve the problem by a review of the lineage of all Lewis families in Llantilio Pertholey; she discovered that there were three seated there at the period with which we were dealing. First, there was the family of John Lewis (from Richard Lewis of Llangattuck), in Brecknockshire, who bore as his Arms: <u>A dragon's head erased vert</u> <u>holding in its</u>

mouth a Hand gules. This is the Arms of Rhys Goch from whom Richard Lewis descended and they are the arms engraved on the tombstone of John Lewis in Gloucester, Virginia. The second Lewis family was that of Llanaply Parish who carried as their arm Argent, a Bear Sable. This Coat has never been associated with our family arms, so it was obviously not the family of Johane Lewis. The third family investigated was that of Llanddewi Rhydderch—their arms being quite distinct from the other two families, being Three leopards faces on a chequy fesse.

However, the arms of the last-mentioned family are quartered on the East window of the Parish Church of Llanddewi Rhydderch and are there quartered with the arms of "de Trevely" (Azure three plates) which had been acquired by them through intermarriage with an heiress of the de Trevely family of that parish. These Arms were borne by Sir Walter de Trevely who came into Wales with the Norman Conqueror, Bernard de Newmarsh, and at one time owned almost the entire Parish of Llanddewi Rhydderch. These arms were engraved in the fourth quartering of the shield on the tombstone (the position of the wife of John Lewis), and the deduction is that she was a member of the Llanddewi Rhydderch family. After determining which Lewis family Johane Lewis derived from we could move ahead and place her on the Pedigree of the Warner Lewis Family—for, after all, her blood flows in the veins of this Virginia family!

As Richard Lewis was the obvious father of Johane Lewis, wife of John Lewis, the author proceeded to research his background. If he was a member of the Llanddewi Rhydderch family, then he must have come from Lewis ap John Wallis (de Valence), Vicar of Abergavenny and St. Teilo Parish. The most prominent member of this family was one Dr. David Lewis, Judge of the Admiralty under Queen Elizabeth I, Principal of Jesus College when it was founded, and many other high positions. He is buried in the Lewis Chapel of the Church at Abergavenny. He wrote his WILL in 1584, leaving most of his property to his brother William Lewis of Ysgyrid. This family is shown on a chart in Bradney's History, Volume I, Part II, page 285. Besides David and William, there was also listed Richard and Thomas, both of whom were written off as dying without issue. Mr. Baker-Gabb, a member of this family and a capable genealogist, made the same mistake.

Realizing that this family was strongly Protestant and that Dr. David Lewis had been prominent at Jesus College, I perused the Alumni Oxonienses, a reprint of which is in the Library of the Virginia Theological Seminary at Alexandria. On page 909 of same is an entry of one Richard Lewis, "Priest," who graduated in 1558, undoubtedly the father of Richard ap Richard Lewis. Also, on page 909 is another Richard "Lewes" who matriculated in 1581 at 18 years of age, making him born about 1563. This Richard Lewis also received a degree in B.C.L. (British Common Law) "by accumulation" in 1603.

Dr. David Lewis, in his WILL of 1584 named this last-mentioned Richard Lewis as my nephew Richard ap Richard Lewis—clearly identifying the two members of his family in the previous paragraph. He left Richard Lewis an interest in an estate in Llantilio Pertholey, if his niece by his brother William Lewis should die without heirs. The estate, called Porth-y-Park was located in a "dingle" (hollow) between the

Rholben and Deri Mountains. It had originally belonged to the Lordship of Abergavenny, later going to the Catholic Church; then in the dissolution of Catholic lands at the time of the Reformation, it had been bought by Dr. David Lewis, along with other lands and tenements. This former Hunting Lodge contained over five hundred acres. The name means Gate to the Park, and Bradney writes that it remained in the hands of a family named "Lewis" for several centuries. So this is the manner in which Richard Lewis, father of Johane, came into Llantilio Pertholey.

When Richard Lewis was residing in this Parish, he served as "Curate" and "Vicar" of St. Teilo in the years 1612-1614, signing the yearly record of Births, Marriages, and Burials in Latin—which would indicate that he had been trained as a priest. There is no other record of him in the "Register" except that of his death as Richard Lewis, Clerk, buried Nov. 13, 1617. While he was serving as "Vicar" he wrote the death of Gwenllian Howell in the records as at Porth-y-Park on October 16, 1613. This is the only instance where a place of death was cited, and this time probably because Richard Lewis was living at Porth-y-Park with Gwenllian Howell; she was the Grandmother of his daughter Johane, by marriage to John Lewis. There was mention of another member of John Lewis' family at Porth-y-Park. It was in the WILL of Dr. David Lewis when he wrote that one Harry Morgan was "in tenure" at that place—managing it for him while he lived in London. When this Harry Morgan died on October 12, 1627, he was recorded as Harry Morgan Watkin, identifying his father as Watkin Morgan, Gent., grandfather of John Lewis—in other words his Uncle and Brother to his mother, Catherine. When his wife died as Margaret Morgan on November 11, 1629, one can recognize the change from the patronymic system to that of English surnames.

After determining the pedigree and descent of Richard Lewis, father of Johane Lewis, wife of John Lewis the emigrant, the next genealogical problem was to trace the line of Johane's mother—for she, too, had a place on the pedigree of the Virginia family. Only a short time after the death of Richard Lewis his widow married for a second time. On the marriage record in the "Register" for January 18, 1618/19, her first name only is given—as "Johane." We were at a disadvantage in knowing her surname and it would have been completely impossible if it were not for the fact of a comment in Bradney's History, Volume I, Part II, page 200, in which he wrote that "John, the son of John ap William Proger of Wernddu married____daughter to____Lawrence and widow to Richard Lewis." (Sic) This is a most important item, as it gives the last name of the mother of Johane. The marriage record in St. Teilo's "Register" gives her husband as JOHN MORGAN.

The family pedigree concerning whom Bradney made this comment was the Senior Line of the family of HERBERT (going back to the Earls of Pembroke). They had adopted the surname of PROGER, were devoutly Catholic and one branch had broken off with a David Morgan to found the "Triley" line of Llantilio Pertholey. There were several families bearing the name of MORGAN at that time. However, I believe that this is one of the few mistakes of Bradney—and he made few—he confused the John Morgan of Wernddu with another John Morgan equally close to the family of Richard Lewis.

Now that we were informed by Bradney that Johane Lewis' mother was a daughter of a LAWRENCE we could hope to locate her on a pedigree of that family.

Another Morgan Family of Monmouthshire was that of MORGAN OF LLANWENARTH who were descended from Ynyr, King of Gwent, and who bore the same Rhys Goch Arms as John Lewis. The Pedigree of this family is to be found on page 352 of Bradney, and it notes the relationship of this family to an heiress "to lands in Llangfihangel Crucorney" (as was noted in my book). This is the family who were "deforciants" in the law suit that John Lewis presented to the Judges at Westminster over Ty-Hir—they were all "cousins." The pedigree lists one "JOHN MORGAN, son of John, who married (?) daughter and sole heir to Lawrence Jenkin of Llanfoist." With the help of the ancient "Register" of St. Teilo and Bradney's wonderful History we have the complete name of Johane Lewis' mother— JOHANE LAWRENCE! The "Register" listed him both as JOHN MORGAN and JOHN MORGAN AP JOHN, both of which are correct. His children by Johane Lewis were baptized under the last name as Gwenllian on March 11, 1619, Elizabeth on April 25, 1621, and Thomas on March 1, 1622. Johane (Lawrence) Lewis Morgan is recorded in the "Register" as "Johane Morgan Lewis buried February 25, 1622/23." This form of her name fully explains in the patronymic system the fact that when she died she was the wife of MORGAN, but that at the time of marriage to him she had been LEWIS.

Before leaving the Lewis Family of Llantilio Pertholey, the author wishes to make it clear that the final deduction concerning the Pedigree of this Lewis Family was that it was of the same name, the same Pedigree, and the same Coat-of-Arms as that conclusion originally stated. Johane Lewis simply derived from a brother of the William Lewis first brought forth as her ancestor.

Now it seemed wise to pursue the pedigree of the Lawrence Family to which Johane Lewis belonged. The author turned to the Price of Llanfoist family in Bradney, pages 360-361, a family descended from Ynyr, King of Gwent, who were the antecedents of the Lawrence Family we are interested in. One branch settled at Wernddu and another at Llangattuck-nigh-Uske, homeplace of the Lewis of Rhys Goch Line. A very celebrated early member of this family was one *DAVID THE WARRIOR* who fought on the Yorkist side in the War of the Roses and was probably at the Battle of Banbury in the mid-fourteenth century, where it is likely he obtained the name "Warrior." There is a most interesting tomb to this personage at the Church of Llangattuck. Another tomb at this Church belongs to his Great-Great-Grandson, one *OWEN LAWRENCE*, who married into the family of William ap John Philip of Blaengavenny, Llantilio Pertholey, and thus brought that family down into this parish. The brother of this Owen Lawrence was one JENKIN AP LAWRENCE (page 361 of Bradney) whom it states had an only daughter and heir who (sic) *"Married JOHN, son to John ap Thomas MORGAN of Llanwenarth, living 1610."* This clearly identifies the father of Johane (Lawrence) Lewis Morgan as of the family of Lawrence of Llanfoist and her second husband as John Morgan of the family of Morgan of Llanwenarth. The elements of Name, Place and Time are all in accordance. Under this last-mentioned item, Bradney wrote: "vide p. 352" which is the Pedigree of Morgan of Llanwenarth!

The Lawrence Family descended from Sir Richard Bullen who came into

Wales with Bernard de Newmarsh and was granted vast lands. The family remained purely Norman for three generations, and in the fourth they intermarried with the Welsh nobility and became truly Welsh. This was Lawrence ap William (Bullen) from whom the line we are treating derives. Their seat was Dyffym Mawr and one branch settled in Llangattuck-nigh-Uske where Sir William Lawrence was "Portioner" of the Church of Crickhowell in 1569 and Vicar of the Church at Llangattuck during 1573-83. Generation after generation were Protestant "priests." The family started in Dyffryn Tudal (Tudwal's Valley) in Llanddewi Rhydderch, and they early married into the family of de Trevely who were established there. Hence, their use of the Arms of that family, namely Azure three plates. Thus Johane Lewis would have the right to use those arms from both her father (Richard Lewis) and her mother (Johane Lawrence). As both the Lewis of Llanddewi Rhydderch family and the Lawrence family of Llanfoist were so prominent and ancient, it is only proper that he should place his wife's Coat-of-Arms on his shield, remembering also that Johane was "sole heir" to her father, Jenkin ap Lawrence.

Item 2 - In closely studying the "Register" of St. Teilo, I observed another of the Lewis name who had not been identified previously. This was one WILLIAM LEWIS who appeared to be having a family in the early part of the 1600's; his daughter Elizabeth was born in 1605, his son James in 1608, and finally a son William born in 1611. This family does not appear to be of either the Rhys Goch line, or the Lewis of Llanaply family. They most likely were of the Llanddewi Rhydderch family. At this point the author speculated that William Lewis might have been an elder brother to Johane Lewis, wife of John Lewis. If he had married at the customary early age of eighteen years, so prevalent in country parishes, then he was probably born at least by 1585/86. This year was immediately after the graduation of Richard ap Richard Lewis from Jesus College. If this deduction is correct, then the youngest son William Lewis, would have been nephew-by-marriage to John Lewis—the blood nephew of his wife Johane, and John Lewis would have been his uncle—which is a relationship other genealogists in Virginia have assumed before—in resolving the degree of relationship between John Lewis and the "Major" William Lewis who traveled with the former to Virginia, and settled beside him on Poropotancke Creek, and left his lands to John Lewis' two sons. Add to that the fact that this same Major William Lewis named his plantation PORTHOLY—very likely in honor of his place of birth—Llantilio Pertholey Parish! No one has ever ascertained whether the LYDIA who traveled with them in Virginia was the second wife of John Lewis or wife to William Lewis.

Item 3 - In pursuing the relationship of Major William Lewis and John Lewis the emigrant even further, it would be interesting to cover their life together prior to coming to the Colony. Wales at that time was deeply involved in the Civil War of England, and the gentry of Wales was definitely Royalist.

The author was fortunate to have all available copies of the journal published by the Brecknock Society, called Brycheniniog. This County of Brecknock was directly above Monmouthshire, and the identical conditions prevailing at the time of the Civil War would have been current in both. In Volume VIII (1962), page 1, is a most enlightening article by Sir Frederick Rees, formerly Principal of the University College of South Wales and Monmouthshire. He writes: "Opposition to the King had no support among the Gentry. As there was no standing army in the county each party attempted to make what use it could of the local trained bands. They consisted of the able-bodied men who were supposed to be trained at intervals. These militia troops became the nucleus of the infantry of Charles I. The King, at the beginning of the War, by issuing Commissions of Array, and Parliament, by passing the Militia Ordinance, summoned the trained bands to mobilize in the counties over which they had control. The King, after raising his standard at Nottingham on 22 August, and thus formally declaring War, moved towards the Welsh Marches, for he knew that active steps were being taken to raise the infantry of which he was in such great need. Commissioners of Array continued to raise forces during the years 1643 to 1645... The King conferred at Abergavenny with the Commissioners of Array of the South Wales Counties." He then retired to Raglan Castle (Gwent).

The King's War on the Scottish Border is historically known as The Bishop's War. It is obvious from the recruiting practices of the King that the troops employed there by him had been raised in South Wales, mostly. Now there are not many historical documents and accounts extant on the Civil War in England, as Cromwell's adherents saw that most of them were destroyed. However, there is a fine book entitled Memoirs of the Civil War in Wales and the Marches (1642-49) by John Roland Phillips, 2 volumes, London, 1874. This book is difficult to obtain, but the very courteous Librarian at Duke University sent me Xerox Prints of pertinent pages. On pages 375-379 and 396-399 is most valuable material. This material had been published contemporaneously in leaflet form in London. The first one reads: "Esquire Lewis came upon the wall, and speaks to some gentlemen of the country that he knew, and tells them that he was willing to deliver up the Castle upon these terms the Esquire Lewis desired." Col. Ewer (Cromwell's deputy) took prisoners as follows: Esquire Lewis, Major Lewis ... Ensign Lewis. "These prisoners we have put into the Church, and will keep them until I receive further order from General Cromwell." Chepstow, May 25th, 1648.

After Chepstow fell, two other Castles—Tenby and Pembroke were taken. It is the author's interpretation that the "Esquire Lewis" described as being in charge of negotiations with Cromwell's aide was John Lewis, the emigrant, who was at that time Burgess of Abergavenny (appointed "Capital Burgess" by King Charles I in 1639); one of the obligations of that post was to militarily defend the County in time of distress. The "Major Lewis" with him was obviously a part of the Garrison of the Castle, as was the "Ensign" Lewis (the lowest rank of the English Army at that time). The title "Esquire" was only given to an elderly prominent member of a distinguished family.

The "Major" Lewis at Chepstow could very well have been his nephew of Llantilio Pertholey, a professional officer, who after serving as an "Ensign" in the Bishop's War, had during the years between of the Civil Wars risen to the rank of "Major." The Civil War, by Mr. Phillips, on page 3, has a catalogue of the Noble,

Royalist promoters who raised troops for the Bishops' War, and included among them is William Seymour, Duke of Hertford, (South Wales). No doubt young William Lewis, as a member of the gentry, had been given a commission as "Ensign" for that war; for there is an Appendix in the book with the names of all the Colonels, Majors, Captains, Lieutenants and Ensigns, etc., and under the Army List (page 80) in the Regiment of Colonel Henry Wentworth (page 79) one finds the name of Ensign William Lewis. The "Ensign Lewis" taken prisoner with the two older men at Chepstow in 1648 was quite likely David Lewis whose birth was in the "Register" of St. Teilo as the son of a William Lewis. The name David is a typical one for the Llanddewi Rhydderch Family. Mr. Baker-Gabb, in his Collection at the National Library, Document #715, states that these three are undoubtedly Monmouthshire men, and that they do not seem to fit on the pedigree of his Llanddewi Rhydderch family; he also states that the "heir" to the St. Pierre Family—the only other possibility—was "a minor" and it could not possibly be he. Hence, it appears clear that these three men at Chepstow were of the Llantilio Pertholey family of John Lewis.

After being taken prisoners at Chepstow, and exiled to the Barbados for two years according to the Articles for the Surrender of Pembroke Castle 1648 (Document cxvi, K of Phillips)—whereby the officers and gentlemen—"do depart the Kingdom, and not return within two years from the time of Departure." The terms for the other two Castles of Tenby and Chepstow would have been the same. After two years in Barbados John Lewis probably reassessed the situation in England, and seeing no political change, decided to "adventure" in Virginia, where a possible Land Grant was available!

Item 4 - In the Library of Congress is a most interesting book entitled Curt-Gollen and its Families by A. Raymond Hawkins (a Brecknock Museum Publication of 1967). On page eleven of same it has a paragraph stating: "Lewis Morgan granted Arms by the Marquis of Worcester, 1656." This Lewis Morgan was the head of the elder line of the pedigree of RHYS GOCH, the Llangeny Line, of Brecknockshire, Wales. The article states that there is among the "Harley Manuscripts of the British Museum a GRANT made on the 3rd of July, 1656, by Edward, marquis of Worcester, to LEWIS MORGAN and his heirs forever, the right to bear on his shield of arms the Crest of himself (namely, the Marquis and his ancestors) a Dragon's Head holding a human Hand in its Mouth."

On page fifteen of same is the Coat-of-Arms engraved in stone on the tomb of John Morgan in 1675, fourth son to James Morgan, nephew and heir to this LEWIS MORGAN, which is practically identical to the Coat-of-Arms engraved on the tombstone of John Lewis in Gloucester, Virginia. As Lewis Morgan was the head of the Rhys Goch Line (descended from Maenyrch, Lord of Brecknock, and Caradawg Freichfras, Knight of the Round Table), the author would assume that her ancestor, John Lewis, as a descendant of the Cadet Line of the same family, would be entitled to the arms granted to the head of his family, 1656.

Attached to this little book is a "drawing" appended to the Morgan Arms, and a Preamble to the Grant which was addressed more particularly to the College of Arms, whose functions were temporarily suspended during the Protectorate of Oliver Cromwell. The Preamble clearly suggests that the Grant was for some "particular" service. The Marquis of Worcester was the strongest adherent of King Charles I, and no doubt the "service" rendered to him by Lewis Morgan was in connection with the Royalist Cause at that time.

The author wrote to Sir David Wilson, Director of the British Museum, requesting a good copy of this GRANT. The Manuscript Division located it as Harleian Document #1470. It was written in Latin; I am proud to have a copy.

The author wrote to a gentleman who has been exceedingly kind, Sir Walter Verco, Surrey Herald at the College of Arms, and informed him of the existence of the GRANT, in case they did not have it registered at the College.

Item 5 - The generation before Rhys Goch was MAENYRCH, LORD OF BRECKNOCK. He married ELINOR, DAUGHTER OF EINION AP SELEFF, LORD OF CANTREFF - SELEFF. By this marriage the entire County of Brecknock was re-united for the first time in many generations. It also brought into being a Double Line from Caradawg Freichfras, as her father was fifteenth from Caradawg. In the veins of the issue of this marriage flows a double infusion of the progenitor of the line. This was the Brecknock in existence when Bernard de Newmarsh, the Norman Conqueror, arrived in the Welsh territory. (Theophilus Jones, History of Brecknock (1909), page 46.

Grace McLean Moses
McLean, Virginia,
February 6th, 1988

www.ingramcontent.com/pod-product-compliance
Lightning Source LLC
Chambersburg PA
CBHW071112090426
42737CB00013B/2572